Build Confidence

OVER

FENCES!

TAKE THE FEAR OUT OF JUMPING WITH

THIS SIMPLE STEP-BY-STEP PLAN.

By Holly Hugo-Vidal with Sue M. Copeland

PRIMEDIA
EQUINE
NETWORK

First Published in 2005 by PRIMEDIA Equine Network

Practical Horseman
656 Quince Orchard Road, #600
Gaithersburg, MD 20878
301-977-3900
VP, Group Publishing Director: Susan Harding
Editor: Sandy Oliynyk
Editorial Director: Cathy Laws
Director, Product Marketing: Julie Beaulieu

Printed in the USA.

Order by calling 800-957-5813 or online at www.HorseBooksEtc.com

Photographer: Mandy Lorraine
Book Design: Lauryl Suire Eddlemon

Library of Congress Cataloging-in-Publication Data

Hugo-Vidal, Holly.
   Build confidence over fences! : take the fear out of jumping with
this simple step-by-step plan / by Holly Hugo-Vidal, with Sue M. Copeland.
     p. cm.
 Includes bibliographical references and index.
 ISBN 1-929164-30-0 (alk. paper)
 1. Show jumping--Study and teaching. 2. Show jumpers (Persons) I.
Copeland, Sue M. II. Title.
 SF295.5.H84 2005
 798.2'5--dc22
                           2005034616

ISBN: 1-929164-30-0

*I dedicate this book to my
mother, Helen Marrow, who's never
missed a horse show.*

—*Holly Hugo-Vidal*

The authors wish to thank the following people:

- Lyman T. Whitehead, of Eight Fences LLC in Redding Center, Connecticut, the trainer and rider who appears on the cover and in most of the photos in this book, aboard Heir Apparent (gray) and Summertime (chestnut), owned by Margo Stever; and Jaslo (bay), owned by Hunt Ltd., and Blair Hackel-Weiss.

- John Talley, manager of Lyman T. Whitehead's Eight Fences training facility.

- May Boykin, rider aboard Nikki (chestnut), owned by Jack Schmeltzer.

- Jennifer Brooks-Clark, shown aboard her horse, Douglas Fir (black).

- Susan Heller, owner of Call Waiting, pictured on the back cover and bio page with Holly Hugo-Vidal.

- Lucy Mitchell-Innes and David Nash, for the use of their Comfortside Farm in North Salem, New York.

- Carol Molony, lifelong friend and true horseman for her generosity and the use of her Stony Creek Farm in North Salem, New York.

- Julie Beaulieu, Director of Product Marketing for Primedia Equine Group, for her continued support and help in getting this book published.

- Cathy Laws, Editorial Director, Primedia Equine Group, for her "fresh eye" on the words in this book, and her positive and speedy approach to tight deadlines.

- The editors of *Practical Horseman Magazine*, who over the last two decades worked with Holly on the various articles that formed the framework for this book.

- Philip Cooper, Art Director for *Dressage Today*, for his wizardry in Photoshop, and all his time.

- Lauryl Suire Eddlemon, Art Director of this book, for pulling it all together with her usual talent, speed, and professionalism.

About the Authors

HOLLY HUGO-VIDAL

Originally from Westchester County, New York, Holly spent most of her life in Bedford. It was there she met legendary horseman (and current USET Chef D'Equipe) George Morris. Shortly after graduating from the School Of Visual Arts, Holly was prompted by George's methods, high standards, dedication, and integrity to opt for a career in horses, rather than art.

Today Holly's approach to training reflects the influence of the legends with whom she's been associated. With former husband, Victor Hugo-Vidal, she ran the successful show barn Cedar Lodge Farm, in Stamford, Connecticut. It was during that time that Victor's wonderful teaching abilities became a strong influence.

Holly's next mentor came in the form of another legend, Rodney Jenkins. Rodney's unique talent, coupled with his ability to read horses and create in them a desire to please, provided her with invaluable lessons. Holly's experience with each of these great horsemen is reflected in her own methods. She shares with her students George's belief in solid basics and his demand for excellence, Victor's ability to help anyone with a desire to accomplish his or her goals, and Rodney's insight, wisdom, and horse savvy.

Holly lives with her mother in Rancho Santa Fe, California, and operates her Pacific Blue show barn in Del Mar. She works with a small group of juniors and adults with the requirement being a desire to learn and a love of horses. She also judges and gives clinics around the country.

Holly and friend.

SUE M. COPELAND

An award-winning journalist in the equine field, Sue is a life-long horse owner. She was an editor of *Horse & Rider* Magazine, a PRIMEDIA publication, for 11 years. There she garnered numerous awards, including the American Horse Publications coveted General Excellence title for the magazine and its team. In the late nineties, Sue stepped back from the editorship to pursue a freelance career.

She is creator, editor, and co-author of a trilogy of books: HANDS-ON HORSE CARE, which won the AHP's Best Equine-Related Book honor; HANDS-ON SENIOR HORSE CARE; and HANDS-ON DOG CARE. That book was nominated for excellence by the Dog Writers Association of America, and won a Glyph award for Best Book from the Arizona Book Publishers Association.

Sue remains a contributing editor for *Horse & Rider* and its sister publication, *Practical Horseman*. She's campaigned hunters to national honors with the help of such trainers as Shane George, Louise Serio, and Peter Pletcher. CMF Distant Drums, shown with Sue at left, won an APHA World Champion Working Hunter title under the guidance of Peter, with trainer Chuck Briggs in the irons. Sue and "Drummer" compete in APHA and USEF competition. She and her husband, Rick, share a farm in Richmond, Texas, with their dogs and horses.

ACTION SHOTS

Table of Contents

Foreword

I've known Holly Hugo-Vidal for over four decades. Our paths first crossed when Holly came to Secor Farms, in White Plains, New York, to watch me teach. Gordon Wright, my mentor, was based there for several years. I also taught at several private farms in the area; again Holly would be there to watch. I was impressed with her dedication and desire to learn.

In the early sixties, a show barn was built for me in North Salem, New York, called Salem View Farm (today it's known as Old Salem Farm). Holly trained with me there. She was just out of the junior division and briefly showed as an amateur. By the time she turned professional, she was well acquainted with my methods and indoctrinated in the basics.

A short time later, Holly married my long-time friend, Victor Hugo-Vidal. Together they ran the successful show barn, Cedar Lodge Farm, in Stamford, Connecticut. I'd begun my own show barn, Hunterdon, in Pittstown, New Jersey, and our riders competed at many of the same shows. Holly mainly focused on the hunters and equitation, developing young riders from the ground up, and always stressing the importance of basics.

In the late seventies, Holly spent several years with the great rider, Rodney Jenkins. She rode many of his horses at home in Virginia, as well as at the shows prior to Rodney competing on them. One favorite was the well-known Grand Prix jumper, Idle Dice. Rodney also showed horses for Holly and her clients, bringing another dimension to her teaching.

Holly brings her years of experience to this book, and describes her exercises on the flat and over jumps with concise clarity. Miranda Lorraine's photos of Lyman "T" Whitehead (who does most of the riding) clearly illustrate Holly's step-by-step teaching method.

This book, with its inviting approach, will give you the tools you need to be confident and successful. It should be read in its entirety, then later used as a reference. This is a very useful book.

—*George H. Morris*
United States Equestrian Team Chef D'Equipe

Introduction

This method of learning to jump with confidence will work whether you've had experience over fences or never jumped before.

When you approach a fence, do you hold your breath? As your horse covers the last few strides, do you see a distance, or do you see a disaster?

Jumping doesn't have to be frightening. Learning to ride with confidence over fences is like learning to swim with confidence: You may never make the Olympics, but you *can* learn to perform competently, safely, and consistently. After all, riding is supposed to be fun, not a continuing episode of "Fear Factor."

Building confidence is best done systematically, beginning with fundamentals and working logically toward more advanced skills. Even if you've been jumping for years you'll find that revisiting the basics improves your skills. That's why we'll start with a review of your position and flatwork. Fixing problems there is guaranteed to help your jumping.

You'll then graduate to exercises over poles on the ground (even if you've never jumped before, you can do them with ease), before graduating to work over fences.

By the time you've completed the work of the last lesson, you'll be ready to put in a confident—and

By the time you've completed the work of the last lesson, you'll be ready to put in a confident—and competitive— round over a hunter (or any) course. Our progress from first to last will be so gradual and so logical that you'll never have the feeling it's "beyond you."

competitive—round over a hunter (or any) course. Our progress from first to last will be so gradual and so logical that you'll never have the feeling it's "beyond you."

Provided you follow every step along the way, taking no shortcuts, you should never have to feel unsafe or out of control. In fact, since you're going to judge your own progress, there's no reason to do anything you're uncomfortable with.

If you feel over-faced by a new exercise, simply drop back to familiar work until your confidence is

Follow this program faithfully, at your own pace,

and you may never have a bad fence again.

restored. We're not working against a deadline; what's important is that you master every step thoroughly before moving on to the next one. Follow this program faithfully, at your own pace, and you may never have a bad fence again.

WHAT YOU NEED TO SUCCEED

➤ **Your horse:** Your job will be easier and your progress faster if your horse is capable of jumping a simple 2'6" to 3' course with a fairly calm attitude. (This work will improve his jumping performance a great deal, but it's not designed to teach him to jump.)

➤ **You:**

• *Skills:* The ability to control your horse on the flat at all three gaits. Control on the flat is the basis for safe, accurate jumping.

• *Desire:* You *want* to improve your over-fences skills, to boost your confidence (or learn to jump).

• *Relaxation:* A willingness to do less as a rider to achieve more. (You'll see what I mean when we begin this book's lessons.)

• *Focus:* The ability to concentrate on the task at hand, and to visualize what you want to achieve.

• *Dedication:* The work ethic to judiciously follow this program.

• *Determination:* The willingness to persevere, even

when you get frustrated. (And you likely will, as your muscles learn new skills.)

• *Positive attitude:* A willing attitude and an open mind.

• *Gratitude:* A willingness to reward your horse with pats, praise, treats, or a brief break for *any* correct (or incrementally improved) effort he makes.

➤ **Equipment:** A well-fitted bridle, saddle, pad, girth, longe line and whip; protective leg equipment for your horse (if you use it), clean and in good repair. And, if your horse needs them, a pair of spurs and a crop.

➤ **Work area:** A quiet, level work area with good footing, and access to jump poles, cups, and standards.

➤ **Access to a trainer or ground person:** Learning requires feedback. I'll give you tips for recognizing whether you're doing something right or wrong, so you can monitor your own performance. In the beginning, though, it'll be easier to develop self-monitoring skills if you work with someone who can confirm your impressions.

A reputable trainer is ideal. If you don't have access to one, a knowledgeable friend will do. (I recommend you always ride with someone nearby, regardless of your skill level, for safety's sake.) Ready? Let's ride!

Position Check

LEARN HOW YOUR BODY POSITION CAN POSITIVELY—AND
NEGATIVELY—IMPACT YOUR AND YOUR HORSE'S PERFORMANCE
(AND CONFIDENCE), ON THE FLAT AND OVER FENCES.

Before we start riding, I'll review the importance of your position to your horse's performance, be it on the flat or over fences. Your position is the alignment, balance, and independent use of your body parts, from head to toe. Each body part can have a positive—or negative—effect on your horse.

For instance, if you tip your head forward to look down at him, you'll tip your upper body out of balance (and your leg will slip back). If you're not balanced, he can't balance. If neither of you is balanced, your performance—and safety—on the flat and over fences is in jeopardy. That will erode confidence in you both.

By reviewing each aspect of your riding position, you can do a quick "position check" to be sure you're good to go when we start our riding lessons. For that, I'll divide your body into four sections:

I. Legs: from foot to knee.

II. Base of support: your thighs and seat.

III. Upper body: from above your thighs to the top of your head.

IV. Hands and arms: self-explanatory.

Here, we'll look at the correct position for each of those sections. I'll also give you the correct position for the two-point, which you'll use over fences.

I. LEGS

Your lower legs provide the foundation to your position, much like the foundation of a house. We'll start with your foot and work up.

A. FEET

A1. **CORRECT:** Your feet are the anchors of your position. To make them as strong as possible, place the ball of your foot diagonally across the stirrup, with the outside branch slightly in front of the inside branch, as shown. Your heel should be lower than your toe, but not forced downward, which would tense your leg and impair the ankle's shock-absorbing capabilities.

Such a position provides maximum flexibility to your ankle, so it can act as a shock absorber. This also enables you to lengthen your leg, maximizing its contact area with your horse's side, thus improving your balance and security.

A2. **CORRECT:** Your foot angle should mirror the natural way you walk, with your toes turning out slightly, at a natural angle, and your weight evenly distributed across the ball of your foot. That way, your entire inside calf is in contact with your horse's side, for maximum communication and security.

A3. **ERROR—Ball Bearing Weight.** You put all your weight onto the ball of your foot, rather than allowing it to sink down in your heel. This shortens your leg, making it less effective and compromising your security.

A4. **ERROR—Toes In.** You tip your toes inward, putting your weight on the outside of your foot, and pointing your toes directly forward—or even inward. This peels your calf away from your horse's side, again compromising security and communication.

A5. **ERROR—Toes Out.** You turn your toes too far out, so only the back of your calf is in contact with your horse's side. This minimizes lower-leg contact, and also pulls your knee and thigh to the outside, minimizing contact up your leg. There's no way you can effectively deliver aids, and you'll have pinned your position on a shaky foundation.

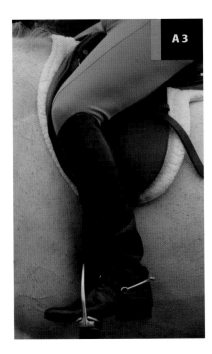

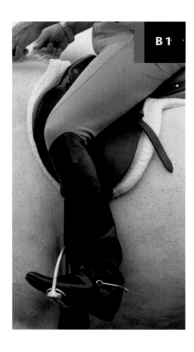

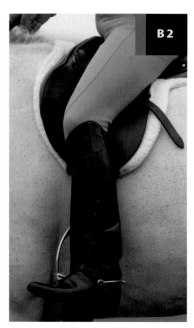

B. CALVES/LOWER LEG

B1. **CORRECT:** To correctly position your lower leg against your horse's side, your stirrup leather should hang parallel to the girth, just as it does…

B2. …when you remove your foot from the stirrup. This will put your calf slightly behind the girth…

B3. …with your heel directly under your hip when your foot is in the stirrup. Positioned as such, your feet and legs are directly under your body, providing a firm foundation of support over which you can balance your weight.

Quick check: *If you look down, you should have to tip fractionally forward to see your boot toe below your knee; it should lie just behind it. If you can see your toe without tipping forward, your leg is too far forward. If a fractional move doesn't reveal it, your leg is too far back.*

B4. **ERROR—Too Far Forward.** If your leg is too far forward, your weight will tip backward. You may end up in a "water-skiing" position—bracing your weight in your stirrups as you're forced to balance on your reins. You'll also be riding behind your horse's motion, making it difficult to jump out of a balanced stride, and putting you at risk of getting left behind over a fence (and jerking your horse in the mouth!).

B5. **ERROR—Too Far Back.** If your leg is too far back, your upper body will tip forward—your weight will be pressing on your toes, rather than into your heels, further driving your seat upward. Your errant leg and forward upper body will send an inadvertent "go!" message to your horse, likely causing him to speed up in an effort to balance beneath you. Plus, you'll weight down his front end from this precarious perch, making balanced flat work and jumping impossible. (From such a position, "chipping" in front of a fence, the term for having your horse add a half-stride before he leaves the ground, is common.)

LEG-POSITION CHECK

With the help of your ground person, practice this simple exercise to develop a feel for the correct leg position.

1. Bring your horse to a halt and rise into two-point position. (See "The Two-Point," page 21.) Have your helper place your leg where it belongs, with the stirrup leather parallel to the girth. Give yourself a moment to let the feeling sink in.

2. Now, have your helper move your foot forward a few inches: Notice that it doesn't take much of a change before you begin to feel as if you're about to plop back into the saddle!

3. Finally, ask your helper to move your foot back several inches. As your leg moves rearward, you'll begin to depend on your horse's neck for support. Try to fix each feeling in your mind so you'll be able to recognize when your legs are out of position, and you'll know what to do to correct them.

C. KNEES

C1. **CORRECT:** To make contact, softly tighten the muscles and tendons of your legs. (If you have long legs or your horse is very narrow, your knees may not quite make contact with the saddle.) With the right degree of soft tension in your legs (enough to hold a dollar bill between your calves and your horse's sides), you'll feel secure without having any effect on his gait.

Quick check: *If your horse speeds up, chances are you're gripping with your legs, rather than maintaining light contact.*

C2. **ERROR—Knee Gripper.** You try to grip with your knees, rather than with your entire leg. This pulls your lower leg off your horse. (See previous comments for the result.)

C3. **ERROR—Knees Out.** You turn your knees out in an effort to cling with your calves. This applies constant pressure, which can desensitize your horse to your aids. You'll also brace your foot in the stirrup, literally pushing your seat up and making balance impossible.

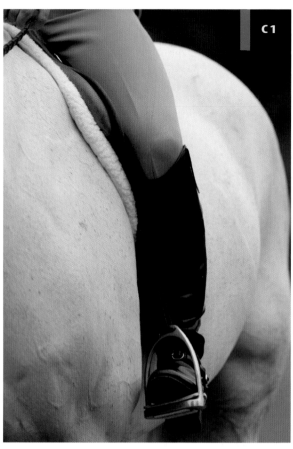

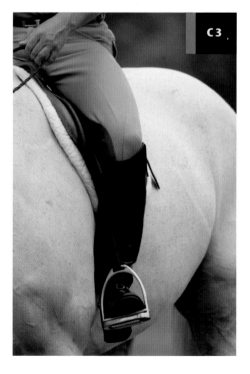

D. STIRRUP LENGTH

D1. **CORRECT:** Let your legs hang loose beside the leathers. The bases of the irons should be level with your ankles. At this stirrup length, the angle between your thigh and upper body will be about equal to the angle behind your knee. This way, when you rise into a two-point (more about that on page 21)…

D2. …your seat easily clears the saddle. (*Note: Many riders shorten their stirrups a hole or two, for jumping. Experiment to see if this works for you.*)

> **TIP**
> If your stirrup length is off by several holes, make the adjustment one hole at a time. This will give your muscles and tendons a chance to adapt, and you'll avoid the insecurity that comes with drastic change.

D3. **ERROR—Too Long.** Your stirrups are too long, meaning they hit below your ankle when you remove your foot. Such a length makes it difficult to attain and maintain a two-point position, which will adversely affect your ability to follow your horse with your body over fences. (You'll know they're too long if it feels as though you're reaching for them.)

D4. **ERROR—Too Short.** Your stirrups are too short. This not only decreases the amount of leg contact you have with your horse, it also jeopardizes your balance, causing you to pop out of the saddle, especially over a jump!

However, it's better to have your stirrups *slightly* too short, than too long. Slightly shorter stirrups can stabilize your calf contact against your horse's sides, making you feel more secure. They may not make your leg look as elegant as the proper length, but you can always lower your stirrups for equitation classes on the flat.

> **TIP**
> If you ride multiple horses, you may have to adjust your stirrup length to accommodate their conformation—and your comfort. For instance, a wide-barreled horse can make your stirrups feel a hole or two short. A narrow, or "slab-sided," horse can make them feel too long.

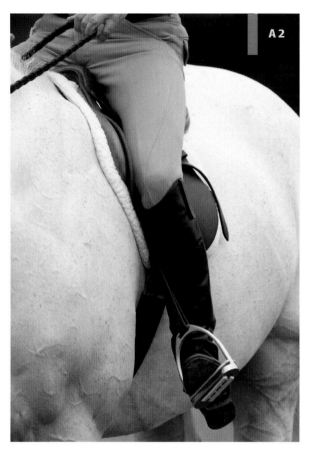

II. BASE OF SUPPORT (Thigh & Seat)

An often-overlooked part of leg position is your thigh. Yet it and your seat are key to your upper-body balance. Plus, any problems in your thigh position can radiate down your lower leg. If your thigh is improperly positioned, it follows that your lower leg will be, too.

A. THIGH

A1. **CORRECT:** Your thigh lies flat against the saddle, with even contact between calf and thigh. (The degree of contact will vary, depending on what you're doing as you ride, but should never be so loose as to allow your leg to swing, nor so tight that your horse perceives the contact as a command to move forward.)

B2. **ERROR—The Thigh Clamp.** You clamp with your thighs. This locks your knees, thighs, and seat, weakening your lower legs, and eroding your security. You also can't effectively deliver aids.

> **TIP**
>
> Concentrate on keeping the portion of your thigh just above the knee in contact with the saddle, and the rest of your thigh will maintain contact automatically.

B. SEAT

B1. **CORRECT:** Sit toward the front of the saddle with your crotch centered directly behind the pommel, so your weight is evenly distributed over both seat bones, then sinks down into both legs, through both heels. *(Note: Your saddle has to fit you or you won't be able to do this: If it's too small, once you have your legs in the right place, your seat will be crowded against the cantle. You should be able to fit four fingers, width-wise, between your seat and the cantle. In a flat jumping saddle, you may be able to make do by allowing your knee to project a little in front of the flap. In a saddle with knee rolls, however, you won't be able to make this accommodation. If you suspect your saddle doesn't fit you properly, consult a reputable trainer or tack shop.)*

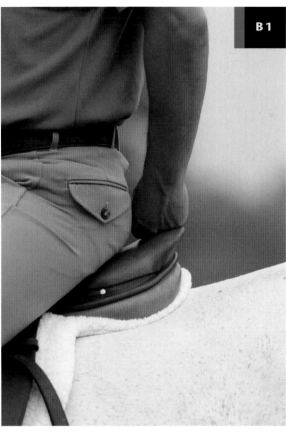

B2. **ERROR—Precarious Perch.** You arch your back and perch in the saddle, with your weight dropping onto the balls of your feet rather than into your heels. This position is often the result of your lower legs being too far back, and makes for a precarious, top-heavy balance point.

B3. **ERROR—Tailbone Trouble!** You collapse your lower back and sit with your seat too far back in the saddle, closer to your cantle than to your pommel. You're sitting on your tailbone rather than on your seat bones. And, your center of gravity is located behind that of your horse, putting you behind his motion. Such a seat position is often associated with lower legs positioned too far forward.

III. UPPER BODY

Just as your feet anchor your position, your upper body works with your seat to serve as your "rudder": Unless you hold your upper body straight, your horse won't travel straight. Many riders carry more weight in one leg than the other without realizing it. To compensate, they lean the opposite way.

For example, if you have a habit of weighting your left stirrup, you're probably leaning to the right. That means your horse is probably leaning to the right, too. On circles and turns to the right, he'll drop his shoulder to the inside, in an effort to balance under your weight.

A. SHOULDERS/CHEST

A1. **CORRECT:** Your weight is evenly distributed over both seat bones and into both legs. Your chest is open and relaxed. Your shoulders are relaxed, too, and rolled back and down, as they align with your hips and ears. That way you can breathe easily, and stay relaxed.

A2. **ERROR—Hunch Back!** You hunch your shoulders, ruining your spine's ability to absorb shock. This also collapses your chest; in an effort to balance, you push back your seat, which pushes your legs forward, causing you to lose contact with your horse's sides. Your balance is wrecked (as is your horse's!). This hunched posture also stiffens your shoulders, which radiates tension down your arms, to your horse's mouth.

A3. **ERROR—The Over-Arch!** When you exaggerate your chest-out posture by arching your back, you can't absorb shock through your seat. That's because you end up tilting your hips forward and sitting on your crotch, rather than on your

seat bones. You'll compensate by trying to absorb shock through your upper body, especially your shoulders. That translates to stiffness—you'll ride against your horse's motion, rather than with it.

A4. **ERROR—Tilt!** Tilting or leaning in one direction with your shoulders is a typical alignment problem. It commonly happens when you turn or use a leg aid, and lack the body control to maintain your balance when doing so. It can also happen when you weight one seat bone/stirrup leather more than the other.

B. HEAD

Are you using your head? It's one of the heaviest parts of your body. As such, it's a powerful tool with which you can direct your horse simply by turning it in the direction you want him to go. When you do so, such as to look at an upcoming jump, you also slightly turn your upper body in that direction, further influencing your horse. You can also throw him—and yourself—off balance, by using your head incorrectly.

B1. **CORRECT:** Your head is balanced atop your spine, and thus your base of support. Your eyes are up, looking in the direction in which you'll be going. Your chin is roughly parallel to the ground.

B2. **ERROR—Eyes Down!** When you look down, you tip your head down, too, which pulls your upper body in front of your base of support, and in front of your horse's center of balance. You can't safely ride to a jump looking down! It's a common error—99 percent of riders who work alone do it. When you ride, focus on objects at eye level in your work area, which will keep your eyes—and your head—up (without tilting your head back).

IV. ARMS & HANDS

Your arms and hands provide a direct line of communication to your horse. A relaxed, elastic feel results in good communication. Stiff, tense arms and hands can lead to a lack of it. Or worse, they can lead to an "argument!"

A. ARMS/HANDS

A1. **CORRECT:** Your elbows are relaxed, slightly bent, and positioned just in front of your body. They act as well-oiled hinges, enabling your hands to follow or resist your horse's head-and-neck movement. Your wrists are straight—not stiff or rigid, but held so your forearm and the back of your hand form an unbroken plane. This provides a direct line from elbow to bit, which is necessary for direct communication with your horse's mouth.

Your hands are just in front of, and on either side of your horse's withers, to allow minimal movement for maximal results. This is where they'll stay—I call it a "fixed hand." It ensures your horse carries the bit in the corners of his mouth, where it belongs. If you move your hands up and down or carry them too low the bit will drop onto the bars of his mouth, causing him to raise his head and fight your contact.

Your knuckles are on the same plane as your wrists and elbows. Any deviation from this straightness, as you'll see, weakens your arm strength and erodes your effectiveness. Your thumbs are the highest part of your hands, and are tipped slightly toward each other. Your fingers are closed firmly enough around the reins so they can't slip through if your horse roots at the bit or trips.

A2. **ERROR—Palms Down, Elbows Out!** Rather than keeping your wrists straight, you stick your elbows out like wings. This automatically turns your hands in and down, which weakens them and your arms, thus your control. You also can't use them to effectively converse with your horse through the bit.

A3. **ERROR—Elbows Too Far Back!** This common rider error means your reins are too long. They should be short enough that slightly flexing or extending your elbow is all that's needed to decrease or increase your degree of contact.

If they're any longer, you'll be forced to bring your hands toward your stomach to make contact, which causes your upper body to tip forward. (Try it as you're reading this, and you'll feel what I'm describing.) All this erodes your ability to make necessary and subtle, balanced adjustments on the flat or over fences. It also adversely affects your control and safety.

THE TWO-POINT

For jumping, your position will stay exactly as I've described it, except that you'll rise into a two-point position. A true two-point, used at a gallop, requires your seat to be all the way out of the saddle. The position I prefer for jumping is a "modified" two-point, in which you raise your seat slightly out of the tack, similar to the position you're in during the "up" phase of a posting trot.

A1. **CORRECT:** Without changing your leg position, bring your shoulders about thirty degrees in front of the vertical, bending from your hips so your seat just leaves the saddle. (Unless you have a tall upper body, your shoulders shouldn't tip in front of your horse's withers.)

You're centered over your horse's center of gravity, with your shoulders open. (By "open," I mean your shoulders are rolled back, with your stomach muscles pulled up toward your sternum). Your pelvis is tipped slightly forward, and your weight is centered over your hips and heels.

A2. **ERROR—Collapsed back!** Avoid bending your waist or rounding your shoulders in an effort to bring your shoulders forward. Doing so will bring your weight in front of your base of support—and your horse's center of gravity. Say good-bye to any hope of balance.

Quick check:

1. With your horse at a walk, rise into the two-point and check the elements of your position. You should feel balanced and comfortable. (You may tire quickly—holding the two-point at a walk is hard work, but a great way to develop strength and balance.)

2. If you fall forward and have to lean on your horse's neck in order to balance, your feet and legs have swung back, behind your base of support. Bring them back to the proper position (as outlined earlier), and try again.

3. If you need your reins in order to keep from falling back into the saddle, your feet have inched forward. (Your upper body might be hunching forward, too.) Review the proper position on page 21, and try again.

4. *Now, pick up the trot while maintaining your two-point. If you're positioned correctly, your seat shouldn't touch the saddle. If it does, your shoulders are too far back; tip them forward slightly, until your seat clears the saddle.*

5. *Next try the canter. During the gait's upward phase, the saddle may contact your seat. However, if it's pummeling your seat (sort of like you're involuntarily posting at the canter), your shoulders have slipped back too far. Bring them slightly forward once more, and tip your pelvis slightly forward, toward your knees, until you feel balanced and in sync with your horse's motion.*

6. *If you feel yourself losing balance, you can always hold your horse's mane to steady yourself, until you build the strength to hold the position. It's far better to reach for a piece of mane than to try to balance on the reins—and your horse's mouth. To do it, hold a length of mane between the thumb and forefinger of your right hand, as shown.*

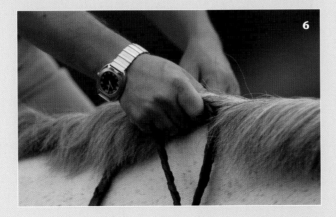

Learning on the Longe

PUT YOUR POSITION IN ACTION, WITH THESE CONFIDENCE-
AND STRENGTH-BUILDING EXERCISES.

How would you like to ride to a fence with confidence, moving in perfect harmony with your horse? You wouldn't constantly be *reacting* to his movements with this aid or that, but rather would be positively influencing him with your body as though you were one. Sound impossible? It's not. You can achieve this feeling with the help of an old friend—the longe line.

You may consider longeing something you stopped needing after your first three riding lessons. Wrong. Riders at almost every level can benefit from lessons on the longe. They provide two absolute essentials for learning:

➤ A secure environment.

➤ Dependable repetition.

Longeing provides other advantages, too. Even the best riders fight a tendency to do too much with their hands. The less skilled a rider you are, the less chance you have of overcoming that natural urge. But longeing wins the battle for you, by taking away all those roles your hands want to play (pull, fiddle, and even balance), giving you other ways to balance and communicate with your horse.

The amount of time all this takes will depend on you—your athletic aptitude, the basic skill level you bring to the program, your natural confidence, and your patience. It could take days, or weeks.

WHAT YOU'LL NEED:

➤ A longe line, longe whip, and side reins.

➤ A snaffle bridle and a well-fitted saddle.

➤ A quiet, trustworthy horse that knows how to longe.

➤ A knowledgeable helper.

➤ A level, quiet area with good footing.

AT THE HALT

1. Outfit your horse in the snaffle bridle, your saddle, and side reins, which will help keep him straight on the circle. Slip the leather end of each side rein over the first billet of the saddle (inset), so it can't slip down past the buckle; snap the other end to the bit below the regular rein. (You want to be able to use your reins without the side reins interfering.)

2. Adjust the side reins so they provide a few inches of slack when your horse carries his head naturally, as shown here. To keep the bit straight in your horse's mouth while he's on the longe line, attach the line by passing the end through the near-side bit ring, up over the top of his head, and down again…

3. …snapping it to the ring on the far side. Place the line an inch or so behind the crownpiece of the bridle; pressure on this point controls his head position more effectively than pressure on the poll does. Knot your reins (inset), catching a piece of his mane in the knot to hold them in place.

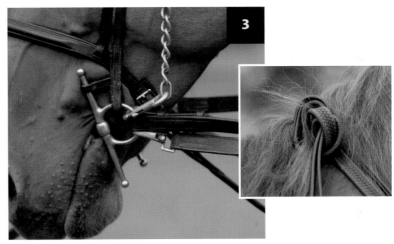

4. Mount up. Have your helper hold your horse, while you establish your position, as outlined in Lesson 1 (page 9). Ask her to confirm the correctness of what you're doing.

You may consider longeing something you stopped needing after your first three riding lessons. Wrong. Riders at almost every level can benefit from lessons on the longe.

5. Now ask her to step back 12 to 15 feet, uncoiling the longe line until she reaches what will be the center of the circle. By keeping the circle fairly small, she'll have more chance of maintaining the shape and rhythm than if it were large. She should keep a consistent feel of your horse's mouth so she can check his pace easily, and use the whip mostly to keep him out on the track (keeping it pointed downward when it's not needed). You're going to take primary responsibility for keeping him moving forward, which will keep you from becoming so focused on position that you lose your effectiveness as a rider.

6. Take up your reins and squeeze your horse into an active walk. Focus on the feeling of weight in your seat bones and stirrups, and on staying relaxed. When you feel secure, you're ready to do some arm exercises that will make a big difference in your ability to balance, especially later when you trot and canter. They'll also show you that you can use your hands independently of the rest of your body.

I've arranged these exercises from least to most challenging, so do them in the sequence I've given you, staying with each one for at least half a lap, or until you feel comfortable with it and your helper confirms that you're maintaining your position.

7. With your hands on your hips, turn your shoulders to the inside of the circle, so they're angled slightly to your horse's shoulders and you're looking directly at your helper. Feel your weight melting down and around your horse's sides, and into your heels. This position should be very comfortable, since you're turning in the same direction as your horse's arc, but be sure you

don't overdo and pull your outside seat bone around with you. If you feel that hip lifting, rebalance your weight over both seat bones.

8. Now turn your shoulders to the outside. This will probably feel a little awkward—you'll be going against your horse's motion—but you shouldn't lose the secure feeling through your hips, seat bones, and legs. If you do, you've probably allowed the movement of your shoulders to extend into your base of support; your helper will probably tell you that your inside knee has come up.

Put it back where it belongs, then hold for several strides. Turn back to center for several strides and repeat until you feel the awkward feeling fade.

9. Now sit centered in the saddle, looking toward the track your horse is on, and cross your arms—first folding them across your chest…

10. …then, after half a lap or so, crossing them behind your back. Your body will naturally seek to balance by sitting deeper in the saddle.

11. Extend both arms at shoulder height. Start by holding them in front of you…

12. …then to the sides, and then to the front again. Each time you open them wide, you'll draw your weight directly over your seat bones and deeper into the saddle.

13. Make large arm circles to the sides in rhythm with the walk. The continuing arm motion will make you focus even harder on maintaining the security in your base. Finish by repeating Step 7.

AT THE TROT

14. Begin your trot work by taking back the reins, squeezing your horse into a quiet trot, and posting with his motion. Focus on keeping your arms relaxed so they stay quiet as your body moves. When you post, lift your seat just enough to clear the saddle and avoid the upward thrust of the stride, no higher. As with the two-point position, a more exaggerated motion will put you ahead of your center of balance and make you insecure.

Stay with the basic posting trot, hands on the reins, until you're dependably posting in rhythm with your horse. When you feel ready to move on to the next step…

15. …come back to the walk and retie your reins. Return to the trot. At first, carry your hands as if they still held the reins. When you and your helper agree that you're doing that well, put your hands back on your hips.

Stay with this work until you've established a truly reliable feel for the trot's rhythm, and for keeping your leg securely under your body. This kind of strong base is always important and never more so than in the sitting trot—the next level—where you'll need to absorb the bouncy motion directly into your body.

To test your readiness, ask yourself and then your helper, "Do I stay with my horse when he loses rhythm or takes a bad step?" If you get ahead of or behind his motion when he slows or quickens, or even pitch forward when he trips, you're following a rhythm in your head rather than feeling the one in his body. Spend more time in posting trot, keeping your hands on your hips and concentrating on the feeling of the motion until you no longer have to think about following it. At this point, you're ready to move on to the sitting trot.

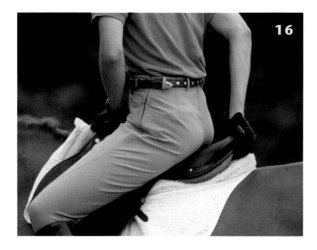

16

17

16. Sitting to your horse's trot is largely a matter of doing less rather than more: of *allowing* your body to follow the motion, and the motion to ripple through your joints and evaporate into thin air. Easier said than done, you say, and you're right.

To stay relaxed you must feel confident, something that's hard to do when the first bounce unbalances you. To overcome fear and give yourself a chance to develop the right responses, you need an adjustment period that guarantees your security—and you're going to give yourself just that by holding the saddle.

Organize your position in the walk. With your friend's help, check that your ear, shoulder, hip, and heel are in alignment. Then take hold of the saddle's pommel with the first two fingers of your outside hand and reach your inside hand behind you to grasp its cantle, as shown above. By doing this, you'll angle your shoulders just enough to put them into alignment with your horse's, the way you had them when you put your hands back on your hips at the end of the walking exercises.

Then, to make sure you're sitting in the deepest part of your saddle (just behind the pommel), use your hands to pull your seat as far forward and down as it will comfortably go. At the same time, keep your joints relaxed so your weight continues to melt down your horse's sides.

17. If you can't seem to pull yourself into the saddle without stiffening, keep your hands on the saddle and raise both legs off your horse's sides, just far enough so they're no longer in contact with him, as our rider is doing, above.

Have your helper maintain the walk while you hold that position for a couple of moments; as you do, your seat will naturally find the deepest, most balanced position in the saddle (and you'll also develop your ability to do different things with different parts of your body).

Then quietly place your legs back against his sides; you'll find the joints in them are more relaxed than before.

18. Keeping your shoulders and elbows relaxed, so your arms don't become rigid, squeeze your horse into a normal trot. As the rhythm changes from the easy-to-sit four-beat walk to the bouncier two-beat trot, focus on the feeling of rhythmically opening and closing your joints to let the motion ripple through them. By staying relaxed, you'll allow the up-and-down motion to repeat itself softly and rhythmically, stride after stride after stride.

19. When you feel comfortable following the rhythm with your body correctly aligned, develop your security by moving your upper body behind (shown), then in front of the motion—without disturbing your base.

Still keeping your hands on the saddle, lean behind the vertical. As you feel your weight roll backward off your crotch and onto the cantle, you'll have to work a little harder to keep your legs in position. You'll want to compensate by bracing forward with your legs—wrong! Say out loud, "Legs back"; then tell your helper when you feel they're in position, having her confirm whether you're right.

Hold this position for at least half a lap. Then come back to the vertical and feel how much easier it is to maintain your base when the rest of your body is in balance with it.

20. Now close your hip angle and bring your shoulders ahead of the vertical by about 25 or 30 degrees. This position is similar to two-point, so it should feel more comfortable than leaning backward. But you'll still have to work harder to keep your legs under your hips and let the motion melt downward than you do when your ear and shoulder line up with your hip and heel.

Keep practicing the sitting trot in your normal position, ahead of the motion, and behind it, until you're equally comfortable in each one. You may need one session or 10 to reach this point, but don't hurry.

You'll be making a valuable investment: developing a strong lower leg and a lasting, reliable base of support for maintaining your balance.

If your balance is too far gone, don't push the panic button; hold the pommel and ask your helper to make your horse walk. Then reorganize your position and try again. Take hold of the pommel with your outside hand, pull your seat forward and down, bring your shoulders back, and get your weight back in your heels.

(Eventually you'll reach a point where you won't need the emotional security of the pommel; by just bringing back your shoulders and deepening your heels—two simple movements—you'll put yourself in balance again.)

21. When you're secure in these exercises, begin to wean yourself from holding on—one hand at a time. First remove your inside hand from the cantle and place it on your hip, where it will help keep your weight centered over your base. Focus on melting into the rhythm, and ride this way until you're confident; then let go of the pommel. (You can reach for it as necessary, until you find your balance.)

22. With your hands first on your hips, then carried as if you were holding the reins (inset), focus on the rhythm and on staying relaxed.

23. If you begin to bounce, your weight isn't in your seat; you've locked your joints and pushed it back up, out of the saddle. Remember, you want enough feel with your calf and inner-thigh muscles to keep your leg steady and effective, but not so much that you freeze the joints. You shouldn't, for example, have as much grip above the knees as you'd have cantering in two-point toward a jump.

Then, focusing on the balanced feeling you memorized earlier, gradually release your hold on the pommel and return your hand to your hip. If you find now that your horse is hard to keep going, you may have pressed him so firmly and repeatedly that he stiffened. Have your helper use more whip so you can use less leg and stay focused on mastering your balance.

24. When you feel ready, drop your stirrups. Make the transition a gradual one. It's easier to work without reins than without stirrups, so when you remove your feet from the irons, hold the loop of the reins with your outside hand as a security blanket.

At first, leave your feet free for just 10 strides at a time, then put them back in the irons for another 10, gradually extending the time as you feel secure. Most riders initially react to no irons by working too hard to

Stretch down into their legs; they lose their balance to the left or the right, wherever they put more pressure. If you do, hold the pommel with your inside hand, and pull yourself back in balance. Then focus on doing less rather than more, feeling for the rhythm rather than pushing into your legs.

25. When you feel secure enough to let go of the pommel, put both hands on your waist. Slowly and quietly begin the arm exercises you used in the walk: Stretch them out in front and open them to the side; make arm circles in rhythm with the stride. The exercises will deepen your feeling for the middle of your horse and make you focus on the tools that provide security, rather than on security itself.

When you take back your stirrups, focus on maintaining the tighter leg and deeper seat that you've developed while working without them. Your stirrups will probably feel very short; if you're uncomfortable, lengthen them a hole. Keep mixing up work with stirrups and without, so you're equally comfortable with both. Just as you don't want to depend on stirrups for security, you don't want to become so used to working without them that you have difficulty when you must use them.

AT THE CANTER

26. Don't attempt the canter on the longe until you feel really secure at the sitting trot. Your horse's ability is a factor, too: If he has trouble keeping his balance in the canter on the longe circle, his rhythm will vary and he'll be harder to ride. If your helper can't get him to maintain a slow, steady gait you feel comfortable with,

SITTING TROT—WORTH A LOT

If you're wondering whether the sitting trot is worth all the work, believe me, it is. Better than any other exercise, it will develop your ability to get down in your tack, to feel and follow your horse's motion, and to become a truly secure rider. The more insecure you are, the more likely you are to use stirrups as a crutch and to depend on them so much that you don't learn to feel the motion.

For that reason, I typically have riders take their feet out of the stirrups and focus on the feeling for 10 or 15 minutes, then pick them back up again. Even if you're pretty much of a beginner, you should spend at least a few minutes without stirrups at a sitting trot: not so much time that you slide all over the place, but enough to begin absorbing the feeling. Gradually you'll be able to do more and more.

26

forget canter work for now and just continue developing your security at the walk and trot. The benefits will spill over to the canter work you do off the longe.

You'll follow the same sequence of steps at the canter that you did at the trot, so you don't ask for too much at one time. Have your helper make your horse's job easier by letting out the longe line 5 or 6 feet to enlarge the circle, and your job easier by keeping him in as slow and rhythmic a canter as possible.

Begin with your feet in the stirrups but both hands on your hips—or hold the pommel with your outside hand if you find you're still a little insecure. When you're comfortable doing this (and aren't leaning forward, as our rider is, or backward, to maintain your balance)…

27. …drop your stirrups and put your outside hand on the pommel. Stay with that until you're confident. Then progress to no stirrups and hands on hips.

28. Once you're as secure with no hands and no stirrups as in all the earlier phases (this may take days—or weeks) finish up the canter phase by taking back your stirrups and rising into two-point position, while keeping your hands on your hips. This is a valuable preparation for our upcoming work over fences.

Even the best riders fight a tendency to do too much with their hands. The less skilled a rider you are, the less chance you have of overcoming that natural urge. But longeing wins the battle for you, by taking away all those roles your hands want to play (pull, fiddle, and even balance), giving you other ways to balance and communicate with your horse.

Flatwork Fundamentals

READY TO JUMP? HOLD YOUR HORSES—THE KEY TO CONFIDENCE
AND SUCCESS OVER FENCES IS IMPROVING YOUR ABILITY TO
CONTROL YOUR HORSE'S PACE AND DIRECTION ON THE FLAT.

I know you're eager to start jumping. But hang with me—even if you consider yourself an experienced rider, you'll benefit from the flatwork I'm about to give you. It's all geared toward making your rides over fences easier for you and your horse. In fact, if you use my flatwork fundamentals, you'll find jumping courses to be like flatwork with fences on your track.

Speaking of…did you know there's a track in your ring? And, that whenever you ride, whenever you school, whenever you jump a course, you should be on it? Your track can be anything from the straight line down a rail, to a circle, to a complicated round of jumps. In other words, it's the predetermined path you take, at the gait and pace you've decided on, wherever you ride.

When your horse is "on track," he's going where you want him to go, at the pace you've determined, with his hindquarters following his forehand. He's accepted your contact and is balanced beneath you, framed between your hands and legs.

If your horse isn't on track, you might notice some of these problems:

➤ He may raise and lower his head.

➤ Evade the bit by overflexing.

➤ Lean on one rein going around turns.

➤ Speed up and/or slow down whenever *he* chooses to.

➤ Canter to fences unbalanced, causing you to put in a bad distance because you feel out of control.

In the next few lessons, I'm going to teach you how to change all that. You'll learn how to see the track, and how to keep your horse moving rhythmically, without speeding up, slowing down, or losing impulsion.

And you'll learn to help him maintain his balance so he's right beneath you, rather than falling in, bulging out, or hanging on your hands. As a result of your newfound control, you'll feel confident and relaxed.

In this lesson, I'll use a simple circle to introduce the essentials of rhythm, balance, and the track. By the end of it, you'll be able to establish and maintain a predetermined, symmetrical, circular track, with your horse slightly bent from nose to tail, on light contact, at a nice, active, posting trot. When you've mastered the circle, you'll have made the giant step toward moving him in balance, in rhythm—and keeping him right where you want him, all the time.

WHAT YOU'LL NEED:

➤ A well-fitted saddle (for this and every lesson going forward).

➤ Bridle with a smooth-mouth snaffle. (If your horse pulls, try a slow-twist; the flatwork we'll do here will help you get him back to the milder bit for future lessons.)

➤ If your horse is the quiet type, spurs and a stick (for this and all future lessons).

➤ A martingale, *only* if you have a green horse that might throw his head and hit you in the face (for this and all future lessons).

➤ Four cones, flower boxes, or standards (cups removed, for safety) to use as markers.

➤ A review of the previous position lessons.

CIRCLE:
Establishing the track

The circle is the simplest, most basic school figure in riding. Perhaps the real reason I like it so much is that my approach to riding has always been to keep things basic and simple.

Even your horse will like circling, because it naturally encourages him to track under with his inside hind leg, on a figure he can't help but understand because he always returns to the same place.

STEP 1:
LEARNING TO SEE THE CIRCLE

There's no arguing about the perfect track of a circle—it's round, not egg shaped or oval. Still, you'd be surprised at how many times I see a rider let her circle get smaller without being aware of it, or end up 30 feet off the figure and not know how or why she got there.

That's why I want you to train your eye to the track on this simple figure. It has a fixed dimension, be it 30, 40, 60, or 100 feet in diameter. And the circle is very easy to set up with visual reference points, as shown in the diagram above. These reference points

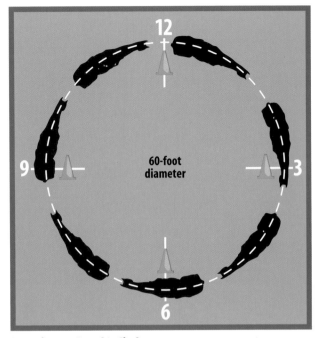

60-foot diameter

Learning to See the Circle

will help you develop your ability to visualize the track you'll be riding.

Here's how to do it: Before you mount up, walk out to your work area. Envision the 60-foot circle you'll be riding as the clock face shown. Divide it into quadrants by placing four equidistant cones or other markers just inside the track at 12, 3, 6, and 9 o'clock. (If you have more markers, you can place them around the circle, too—say, at every point of the clock face.) You can also add another focal point by setting a marker in the center of the circle. Now, let's ride!

STEP 2: RIDING FROM POINT TO POINT

1. Mount up. Establish an energetic posting trot. Track right on the circle's perimeter, passing just to the outside of each marker.

2. Part of being on the track means not only that you steer your horse to follow the figure, but that his body conforms to it. On this circle to the right, he should be bent slightly to the right, from nose to tail. To get that bend, position your right leg at the girth and your left leg a little bit behind the girth.

Although your legs do most of the work to keep

your horse on the track, your reins come into play, too. Close your inside hand while maintaining contact with your outside hand to produce a correct, soft bend through your horse's neck, as shown here. To make steering easier, maintain even contact on both reins. Contact is also very important as a prelude to other work in this lesson, such as maintaining rhythm and keeping him balanced. It will help your horse to flex and soften his jaw. But first things first: At this point in the session, as you're just starting to establish your figure, don't worry if his head is a little bit in the air. It'll come down as the work progresses.

3. If he bulges his shoulder to the outside on the circle, resist the temptation to pull the inside rein, as this rider is doing (above). Doing so would merely over-bend his neck, allowing his shoulder to continue to bulge. (Compare this horse's bulging body position to that in Photo 2.) Instead, bring both reins slightly to the inside as you apply light outside leg, to push his shoulders back into alignment with his body. Avoid crossing your outside hand over his withers, which would wreck his alignment.

4. As you circle, keep your head over your shoulders and your chin level. Help your horse to stay on the figure by focusing your eyes at eye level on the track ahead. As you approach one cone or standard, look beyond it to the next, and so on. When you do so, you subliminally guide your horse, reducing the need for conscious aids. This relaxes him—and you.

GETTING RIGHT WITH RHYTHM

Along about now, you may be approaching mental overload. You're thinking about visual points of reference, the symmetry of the circle, the bend, your position, and the track. As a result, you may lose the impulsion of your trot, *and* the rhythm that goes along with it.

Rhythm is the regularly repeated pattern of your horse's hoof beats as he moves along; it's an indicator he's moving *forward*, not sucking back, ignoring your leg, or oblivious to your hand. Establishing a rhythm goes a long way toward helping him to stay balanced, and therefore toward helping you keep him on the track you've chosen.

Your horse's trot should feel and sound as consistent as a metronome: "one, two, one, two, one, two." Can you hear that? You have to learn to be able to recognize the rhythm and know when it's faltering. One of the most effective ways to school your ear and seat to a consistent rhythm is to practice changing the rhythm. Here's how:

5. Establish a brisk, forward trot.

6. Sit the trot and ask for a downward transition to the walk, using light pressure from your seat, then closing your hands.

7. Walk for several strides…

instantly responsive to your aids. *And* until you can hear and feel the difference between an active trot and a slower, sitting trot, and can effortlessly maintain impulsion and the one-two pattern at either speed.

THE BEAUTY OF BALANCE

You've established the circle, you're maintaining contact with your horse's mouth, and you're controlling the pace at which he travels. Now it's time to put in place the final element of keeping him on this basic track: keeping him balanced. How do you know whether your horse is balanced?

10. His body is straight, with his hind legs stepping in the same path as his forelegs.

8. …then softly close your legs and encourage your horse back into the trot, but at a slower pace. His feet will still be hitting the ground in a "one, two, one, two" pattern, but there will be more time between the beats. You'll have slowed down the rate at which he's moving his legs.

Slower doesn't mean pokey or lifeless. Keep the impulsion no matter how slowly your horse is moving his legs, by pressing him into your rein contact with your legs. (If you're having trouble sitting the trot, trot slow and post.)

9. As soon as you start to lose either your seat or the impulsion and regularity of the gait, post and push him on into the more active trot again. Repeat this posting/sitting/posting transition until your horse is

11. He's working off his hind-quarters, with his topline soft and round, and his shoulders elevated…

BACK IN BALANCE

Here's how to fix some typical balance problems:

➤ **The problem:** Your horse stays on the track for four or five steps, then leans in and makes the circle smaller. (You'll know this is happening because you'll miss a cone or standard, and he'll feel heavy against your inside rein and leg.)

➤ **The fix:** Maintain contact with both reins and both legs. On a circle to the right, use your right (inside) leg to push him back out to your left (outside) rein, which will realign his body. He may continue to lean and refuse to move off your leg, so don't hesitate to use your spur as reinforcement. (Tap him once with your spur; if he ignores that aid, tap him again, harder. Avoid spurring him with every stride, however, or you'll deaden him to your aids—and he'll get mad.)

Avoid getting frustrated if your horse leans in frequently. Instead, think of these incidents as opportunities. The more your horse falls off the track, and the more you return him to it, the better you'll be at predicting how he's going to get imbalanced, feeling when he's imbalanced, and correcting him.

➤ **The problem:** Your horse stays on the track, but becomes heavy on the forehand and leans on your hands.

➤ **The fix:** Get him off his forehand and your hands, but not by having a pulling match (he's guaranteed to win that tug-o-war). And, not by being tough or losing your temper. You do it by using less hand and more leg.

That doesn't mean I want you to pitch your reins away. If your horse is resisting you with six pounds of pressure from his mouth, you'll have to resist him with six pounds of pressure—BUT you'll do it while applying 10 pounds of leg pressure.

This will compress his body into the bit barrier, elevating his shoulders and shifting his weight rearward, over his hindquarters. That, in turn, will ultimately lighten the load in your hand.

The *instant* you feel him soften even slightly, reward him by slightly relaxing your hand while maintaining contact, with an elastic feel. Continue until he's at the speed you want. As soon as he leans on you and speeds up again, resist again. Keep giving and taking, until your horse is carrying himself lightly, in your hand. To further lighten him, see "Ask, Tell, Make," on page 47.

12

diagnostic tool for testing balance. Any time you miss a cone, any time your horse wanders off the circle, or any time you can't ride your figure accurately, *he's not balanced*. For what to do to get him back in balance, see "Back In Balance," page 45.

A Final Word: The Uses of Adversity

These exercises are basic building blocks. Doing them well is going to be challenging, hard work for you and your horse. You might get flustered trying to anticipate what he's going to do and where. You might freeze up in your arms and legs. Your joints could get straight and locked. You might lose the ability to use your hands and legs independently. You might latch onto his mouth.

He, in turn, might start pulling, getting quick, dying underneath you, or hollowing his back and sticking his head in the air. Avoid getting frustrated or discouraged, and above all, don't get mad. Be patient. You're training your horse. Whether it's good training or bad training, everything you do goes directly into his memory banks.

So accept your horse's resistance as input. He's telling you, in the only way he can, to relax and be supple and elastic. He's saying, "Keep your posting clear and regular. Bend your elbow and use it as a hinge. Above all, get down in your heel, soften your ankle, sit up, and use your arms and hands independently if you want me on the track, in rhythm and in balance."

When you get that kind of conversation going with your horse, you're ready to move on to the next lesson: Canter-balance.

13

12. …not inverted, with his head sticking up in the air…

13. … and not leaning on his forehand, so he pulls your shoulders out of the sockets or the reins out of your hands, as this horse is.

You may not feel all the subtle signs of a lack of balance at this point. That's okay. Your track is the ideal

ASK, TELL, MAKE

Transitions are my exercise of choice for lightening a horse that's heavy in your hand, just as they were for testing rhythm earlier in this lesson. However, in this case I want you to take the transition a step further, using an "asking, telling, making" progression:

A. When you feel your horse get heavy and downhill, sit the trot for a stride or two and "ask" for a walk transition by closing your hand.

B. If you get no response, "tell" him to walk with hand plus arm—by bending your elbow and using it as a hinge—and by using your voice quietly.

C. Is he still tuning you out? "Make" him walk by bending your elbow hinge, sitting deep, stepping into your heels and leaning behind the vertical in a combination of hand, arm, and body weight. He will walk, but the walk isn't the issue; the softening, lightening effect of the transition is.

As soon as your horse walks four or five steps (in a nicely active, rhythmic, balanced stride), ask for a forward, rhythmic, active posting trot again. After about 15 steps ask again for the walk, and so on around the circle.

Gradually reduce the degree of your aids by tuning down from "make" to "tell" to "ask," until he's light in your hand, relaxed, using his hind end, responsive, staying on the track, no longer running downhill, and walking when you even "think" walk.

Canter-Balance

LEARN TO SEE (AND KEEP) YOUR TRACK AT THE CANTER WHILE
KEEPING YOUR HORSE RHYTHMIC AND BALANCED—A SKILL THAT'S
CRITICAL FOR CONFIDENCE WHEN JUMPING.

**Bonus: Teach your horse to counter-canter for improved
balance (and improved lead changes).**

With the past few lessons under your belt, you're able to recognize and follow a track (predetermined path) at the walk and trot—just as you'll need to do at the canter when we begin work over fences. You're able to keep your horse relaxed and going forward all the while, in rhythm and in balance, because you're sitting quietly in the middle of your tack with elbows relaxed and hands keeping the contact, following without interfering.

You'll begin this lesson by learning to keep your horse on a circular track, in rhythm and in balance, at the canter. Does this sound too basic? It isn't: If you can't retain his rhythm and balance on a simple circle—no speeding up or slowing down, no drifting in or drifting out—there's no way you'll be able to do it over fences. Next you'll improve that canter—and prepare your horse for flying changes (or improve his current ones)—by working in counter-canter (say, tracking to the left on a right-lead canter, or vice versa).

After your canter-circle and counter-canter work, you'll graduate to our next lesson: Learning to canter a figure-eight pattern over a ground pole, then canter four poles on a circle. All this will prepare you to follow more complex patterns over ground poles. Then we'll be ready to take the confidence you've built with your flat work, and apply it to work over fences.

WHAT YOU'LL NEED:

➤ A level work area with good footing, large enough to accommodate a 60-foot circle.

➤ At least four standards (cups removed, for safety) and/or cones, to use as markers.

Cantering on the Circle

Before you mount up, start by clearly marking a 60-foot-diameter circular track. (A 60-foot circle is large enough to accommodate even a green or stiff horse at the canter.) At first, mark your circle by setting cones or jump standards at 3, 6, 9, and 12 o'clock, as you did in Lesson 3 (see diagram, at right). You'll use these markers to be sure you stick to your predetermined path. Once you've practiced your canter circle for a few days, remove the markers so you learn to stay on track by using your eye alone.

Warm up by walking, then trotting around your circular track, from marker to marker, to establish your eye's ability to follow the track. Keep your head and eyes up, focusing immediately on the upcoming marker once you've reached the previous one.

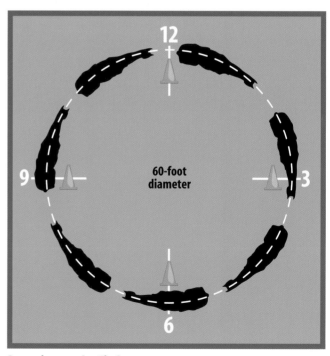

Cantering on the Circle

1. When your horse is relaxed and listening to your aids, pick up a left-lead canter. Keep your inside (left) leg pressing lightly at the girth, with your outside leg about 4 inches behind the girth, as you maintain light contact on your outside (right) rein, to support him on the circle's perimeter. Keep your inside hand soft and following, taking contact only when you need to keep your horse looking in the direction he's going.

And, don't be surprised if you bump up against any or all of these common problems:

➤ **You feel rushed.** Your markers come up much faster than at the trot, so you find yourself "scurrying" with your eyes to spot them at the last minute, and generally feel less organized than at the walk and trot.

➤ **Your horse speeds up.** Your horse's adrenalin kicks in and you end up moving faster than your predetermined pace.

➤ **Your horse cuts in.** Your horse follows his natural tendency (and you follow most riders' natural tendency) to gradually cut in on the circle, making it smaller and smaller.

Handling the first two problems is easy: Adjust your eye to the faster gait by looking farther ahead than you did at the trot. For example, as soon you've established a track to marker 2 (and well before you actually reach that marker), you should be looking ahead to marker 3.

2. If, after you've gotten more organized, your horse is still rushing around the circle, squeeze your fingers to take a stronger feel of his mouth with each stride. Simultaneously bring your shoulders *very slightly* back, so your weight helps slow him down. (If you lean forward, he'll go faster in an effort to balance under your weight.)

Correcting the third problem, cutting in, is no harder. Begin by making sure your contact is steady, with fingers closed firmly on the reins, elbows relaxed, and arms soft and following. Next, increase your inside leg pressure; that leg must not only ask for the bend but also combat the centrifugal force that tends to pull your horse inward on the circle.

At the same time, keep your inside hand soft and flexible as you take a firmer, steadier feel in your out-side rein. Just remember the rule "inside leg to outside hand," and from now on make it a point to ride every curve and turn by that rule. You'll need it not only for the more difficult exercise patterns to come in our next lesson, but also to follow the smooth, bending track that will set up perfectly straight approaches to your lines on course.

When your horse consistently remains balanced and rhythmic (not speeding up or slowing down, nor fading in or out on the circle) at a canter to the left, reverse direction and canter the circle to the right. When you feel ready, graduate to Exercise 1 (next page).

EXERCISE 1:
COUNTER-CANTER SERPENTINE

Here's a simple serpentine exercise to introduce you to the counter-canter. It involves simple changes of direction—without changing leads—at the canter. (See diagram at right.) The counter-canter teaches your horse to carry himself in balance—a key to staying on track. As such, it's a valuable exercise for him whether he's a hunter, jumper, or eventer.

Bonus: That balance will make flying changes easier for both of you. (For more about flying lead changes, see page 61.)

3. Tracking left, ride a left-lead canter along the rail. Just after you turn down the long side of your ring, leave the rail and ride a diagonal path to the quarter line (shown here).

4. Once you get to the quarter line, ease your go-left cues, while maintaining the leftward bend, and squeezing your right leg behind the girth to reinforce the left lead.

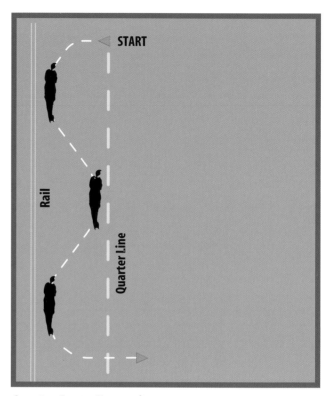

Counter-Canter Serpentine

5. Canter for several strides, maintaining your right-leg pressure as you keep his shoulders in straight alignment with the rest of his body. Then open your right rein two or three inches to "lead" your horse very gradually back to the rail.

6. As he travels to the right to return to the rail, he'll still be on the left lead…

7. …meaning he'll be counter-cantering. If, as you counter-canter back to the rail, your horse tenses up and shortens his stride, anticipating a lead change, avoid tensing your hands and body. Instead, keep your right leg on his side, and maintain soft left-rein contact, to say "left lead, please."

When you reach the rail, release your aids, then repeat if you have room. If not, canter around the short side of the arena, then repeat on the opposite long side, until your horse remains relaxed, drifting off and back to the rail in response to increasingly subtle aids. When he does, reverse directions and repeat on the right lead.

EXERCISE 2:
COUNTER-CANTER HALF-TURN

Once you're comfortable with Exercise 1, you can make the counter-canter more demanding by actually maintaining the lead through a change of direction. In this instance:

A. On a left-lead canter, travel to the center line, rather than the quarter line (see diagram at right)…

B. …and make a gradual turn to the right when you reach the arena's short side. Keep your horse's front end straight, while applying right leg pressure, to move his hindquarters slightly to the left, which will make it easier for him to keep the left (counter) lead.

C. Continue around the short side of the ring, staying on the left lead. Keep the canter slow, sit still, stay relaxed, make sure you keep a feel of both sides of your horse's mouth, and you should be fine.

D. Go across the diagonal to change directions…

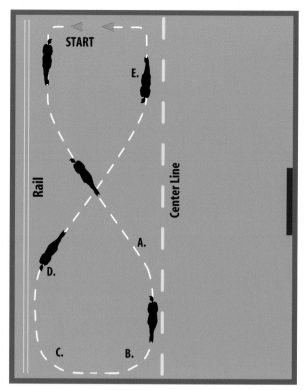

Counter-Canter Half-Turn

E. …then reward your horse by allowing him to canter around the arena or work area on the "correct" lead. Repeat the exercise, then practice your counter-canter on the right lead.

COUNTER-CANTER TROUBLESHOOTING TIPS

Here are some common problems you might face, and how to fix them.

➤ **Your horse breaks to a trot.** If your horse breaks to a trot when you change direction, say, when on the left lead turning to the right, add more right leg when you ask for the turn.

➤ **He changes leads.** If he does a flying change, or he changes in front, correct him by coming back to the walk, moving him away from your inside leg, so you displace his haunch to the lead side. Then pick up the counter-canter again.

Next time around, make sure you aren't dropping your contact on the left rein, make your turn even more gradual, keep your right leg working, and be sure you're sitting in the middle of your horse. (If you throw your weight to the right, because you're heading in that direction, any reasonable horse will swap to the right lead to balance himself underneath you.)

If he keeps trying to switch leads, keep correcting him—quietly. Avoid letting your emotions dictate your response, so you start pulling on his mouth. Losing your temper is not productive; it produces a nervous and defensive horse.

Pole Power

DO YOU HAVE A TENDENCY TO FUSS AT YOUR HORSE BEFORE
A FENCE, MAKING FOR UNCOMFORTABLE (AND CONFIDENCE-ERODING)
DISTANCES? THIS LESSON WILL PROVIDE THE ANTIDOTE!

The goal of our work together is to make you a better rider over fences, right? Well, what poisons your performance over fences is making last-minute changes and adjustments before the jump. Those adjustments disturb your horse's balance. He sees the jump and prepares himself. Then, at the last minute, somebody grabs his mouth or kicks his sides and throws him completely out of rhythm. How can he jump well? How can he stay relaxed?

Luckily for all of us, there's a simple antidote to this performance "poison." And you're well-prepared for it: It involves practicing the skills you've been learning in our previous lessons. You simply sit still, riding the rhythm while maintaining balance and staying on the track. The jump will then "ride" itself.

So let's put all those antidote skills together, by having you ride a figure-eight pattern over a single ground pole, then canter over four poles on a circle. Doing so will enable you to practice keeping your rhythm on track, but with obstacles in your way. With practice, you'll be able to transfer those skills to our upcoming over-fences work.

WHAT YOU'LL NEED:

➤ A level work area with good footing, large enough to accommodate a large figure-eight maneuver.

➤ Four ground poles.

➤ Four cones, to use as markers (optional).

➤ Four pairs of standards (cups removed, for safety).

EXERCISE 1:
FIGURE EIGHT OVER A POLE

First, let's define your track. It's going to be a figure eight, with a ground pole at the center and a rather elongated loop on either side of the pole. Think of each elongated loop as two diagonals connected by a half-circle. To give yourself plenty of room to look ahead on your track, make the distance from the ground pole to the half-circle at the end about 75 to 80 feet—six or seven cantering strides. (You may want to use two or three cones or standards to mark the track of those half-circles.)

Your ground pole should be parallel to the curved side of your half-circle, so your correct track is a per-fectly straight diagonal line from half-circle (at the end of one figure-eight loop) to half-circle (at the end of

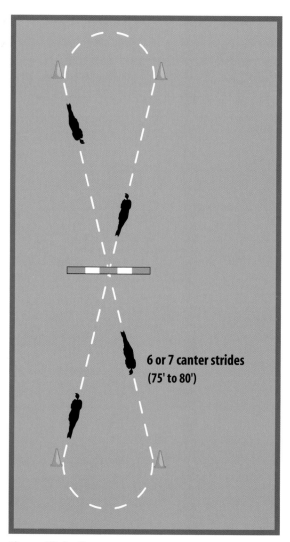

6 or 7 canter strides
(75' to 80')

Figure-Eight Pattern

the other), taking you across the center of the ground pole on a slight angle.

Start at the walk, with your eyes up, guiding your horse along the track and over the pole. Even at this slow gait, focus on maintaining rhythm and balance, sitting centered in the tack, with an elastic, following arm and hand.

1. Next, trot the whole figure, looking ahead and following your track while keeping your horse moving forward in rhythm and in balance. Maintain your posting rhythm, to avoid disrupting your horse's rhythm. And avoid making any changes at the ground pole; just keep posting and let him trot over it.

2. As you navigate the half-circles on the pattern, ride "by the rule"—inside leg to outside hand—to prevent him from cutting in.

3. Once you can follow the track in rhythm and balance at the trot, you're ready to ride the diagonals at the canter. To avoid complicating the exercise with a lead change, you'll drop down to a sitting trot for the turns. Here's how: On a half-circle to the left, pick up the left lead. Exit the half-circle's arc and guide your horse onto the diagonal line. Now, sit perfectly still and maintain his rhythm and balance…

4. …as you cross the pole.

5. Resist the natural temptation to lean forward (shown here) as the ground pole gets closer, which would encourage your horse to quicken or to jump it. You want him to simply keep cantering, as if the pole wasn't there (so in our future lessons he'll keep cantering as if the jump wasn't there, either).

6. If, despite your quiet seat, your horse increases his pace when he spots the pole, as this horse is doing here, simply take a firmer feel on both reins as you approach it, and squeeze your fingers with each stride. Talk to him with a soothing "Whoa-a-a." If you stay calm, after a few repetitions of the exercise he'll calm down, too.

On the other hand, if he sucks back in front of the pole, check first that you're not tensing up and using your hands for balance by pulling at his mouth. Then increase your leg to maintain his canter rhythm up to and over the pole.

7. This rider is demonstrating the simple lead change from right lead to left. Simply reverse to change from left to right.

Once you've crossed the pole, return to a sitting trot a few strides before your half-circle. Plan ahead, look ahead, and think ahead, so you make a smooth transition, then ride a smooth, controlled curving line.

8. Pick up a canter, and ride a diagonal line back over the pole. Repeat, until you can canter the pole with no change in rhythm or balance.

If your horse will automatically switch leads when he crosses a pole (meaning you come out of your left-hand loop on the left lead, and he switches to the right lead over the pole in anticipation of the upcoming right-hand loop), you're ready to try the entire pattern at the canter.

If he doesn't change leads over the pole, continue to change through the sitting trot, as outlined in Steps 7 and 8, as you hone your rhythm and balance skills.

EXERCISE 2:
CANTERING POLES ON THE CIRCLE

For our final exercise, you'll canter over four ground poles set at equal intervals on the circumference of a 100-foot circular track. (See diagram at right.)

9. However, before you set up your ground poles, warm up your horse—and reinforce his responsiveness, which will up your odds for success—with a simpler version of this exercise. Place pairs of jump standards at 3, 6, 9, and 12 o'clock on the circumference of your circle, with enough space between the inside and outside standards that you can pass comfortably between them as you canter your track.

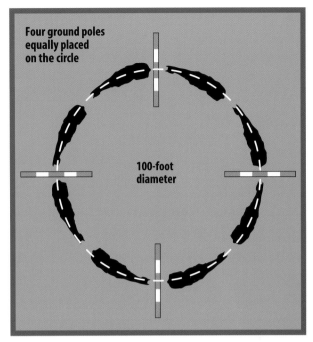

Canter Poles on a Circle

If you find yourself repeatedly coming closer to the inside standards, keep pressing with your inside leg and maintain a firm contact in your outside hand to prevent your horse from spiraling inward. Above all, maintain the rhythm! That steady rhythm is going to be your key to riding to the jumps well in Lesson 7.

You know by now how to influence your horse's pace: Add more leg when he drops below the canter you want; shoulders back and squeezes on both reins when he steps above it. That's the easy part. The difficult part is to pay close enough attention that you catch these pace variations almost before they happen—before your horse has a chance to build up that head of steam, or to fall back into a trot. That takes time and practice.

10. Once you're cantering the circle through your standards at a perfectly even, steady pace, with your horse forward and balanced and your body centered in the saddle in good balance, lay a ground pole straight between each pair of standards, so you'll approach the poles straight...

TROUBLESHOOTING TIPS

➤ **Your horse swaps leads over the pole.** Unfortunately, some horses may switch leads over the poles even though they're circling. If yours is one of these, here's how to keep him on the correct lead: First, ask him to canter as slowly as he can without losing balance and forwardness, so both of you have more time to think about what you're doing.

Close your fingers and relax your arms, so you have a steady feel of his mouth. Then, as you cross each pole, open your inside rein a few inches (move it sideways, away from his neck). Avoid pulling either rein back. (Too much inside rein will make him cut in on the circle; too much outside rein will encourage him to swap leads.) Keep squeezing your outside leg behind the girth to reinforce your lead, and your inside leg right at the girth to prevent his falling in on the circle.

➤ **You look down over the poles.** Avoid the natural temptation toward looking down to check your lead. Keep your eyes up and on the track, and let yourself *feel* that the lead stays true. Above all, don't stop concentrating on your steady pace. If your horse still switches leads despite your efforts, stay on track, come back to a sitting trot for a few strides, then strike off again on the correct lead. With quiet repetition, he'll soon get the idea.

➤ **Your horse rushes or jumps ground poles.** If your horse is an "over-achiever," you'll have to back off from this exercise and start cantering the circle with just one ground pole, at 9 o'clock. As he relaxes and learns to canter quietly over that pole, add a second one at 3 o'clock. When he's quiet over two, add a third pole. Finally, when he's settled and stays in a rhythm over three poles, add your fourth.

You may need days or weeks to get this final exercise right, but stay with it until you do. Why? Because unless you can keep your horse on track in a quiet, steady canter over this circle of ground poles, riding a smooth hunter, equitation, or jumper round will be a virtual impossibility. Remember that cantering a course of fences is no more than cantering a track—in balance and in rhythm with some jumps in the way.

11. …and canter over their centers. Ride this exercise just the way you rode your simple cantering circle through the standards; nothing should change. Your horse's pace should remain as steady and rhythmic as it was without the poles, and you should stay just as relaxed, as you simply continue cantering and turning.

Here are a few specific things to watch out for:
➤ Avoid leaning forward in anticipation of the poles. Just as in your figure-eight exercise, leaning forward can make your horse speed up.
➤ Avoid trying to "see a distance" by fiddling with your hands and legs. Finding the pole is your horse's job; you'll only be interfering.
➤ Above all, don't get anxious and kick your horse at the poles as if they were jumps—they're not. If he leaps over a pole, he'll leap right off your track to the next one!

Concentrate on only three things: keeping your horse active and balanced, keeping his pace (his rhythm) perfectly even, and looking ahead and following the track. And, of course, practice in both directions. Then, if your horse already has his flying changes down pat, you can proceed to Lesson 7: Let's Jump! If not, turn to Lesson 6: Fix That Funky Flying Lead Change.

Fix That Funky Flying Lead Change!

USE THIS S-SHAPED-PATTERN EXERCISE TO TAKE THE
TURMOIL OUT OF YOUR HORSE'S LEAD CHANGES
ON THE FLAT AND OVER FENCES.

Here's a low-key exercise—an S-shaped canter pattern with a flying change you get by *not* asking for it—that will help you and your horse learn to do relaxed, quiet, balanced lead changes without fuss or anxiety. It'll work whether he's a nervous, resistant wreck about changes or a novice you simply want to start as positively and comfortably as possible.

The S-shaped pattern quiets down the whole process: Instead of trying to time the right moment to ask for the change (which tends to make you anticipate, lean, and kick, and make your horse panic and run), you only need to focus on flowing smoothly from one loop of the S to the other, changing his bend as you do it, and letting the lead change just happen.

You're probably saying, "Oh, sure, Holly ....." But without the distraction of timing your lead change, you can concentrate on pace, rein contact, position, the track, and all the other basic qualities. This will keep your horse balanced, rhythmic, light, and ready, so the new bend and the new direction will almost automatically "cue" the change.

And, when the change feels automatic and natural to him, he'll tend not to speed up, slow down, fall in, drop on his forehand, or get nervous and upset. With quiet practice, he'll become so confident and steady on the S that changes will be a snap even in more conventional and challenging locations, such as on the diagonal or after a fence at the end of the ring.

WHAT YOU'LL NEED:

➤ A level work area with good footing, large enough to accommodate a large serpentine maneuver.

➤ Lots of patience. A lack of it will set back your horse's lead changes, the opposite of our goal.

➤ A dressage whip, if you need it.

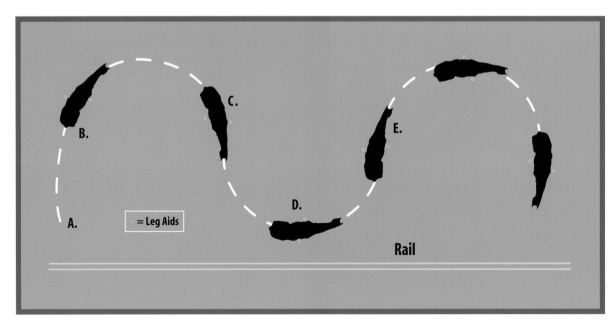

S-Shaped Lead-Change Pattern

Practice at the Trot

You'll begin the lead-change exercise at the trot. Why, you ask? Because it gives you a chance to concentrate on several major components of the exercise—your position and aids, the change of bend, your horse's pace, the track—without worrying about speed.

A. Pick up an energetic trot to the right. Keep your outside (left) leg slightly behind the girth, and your inside (right) leg firmly at the girth, to encourage his body to bend slightly around your inside leg. Feel an equal contact (in ounces, not pounds) on both sides of his mouth, but with your outside hand steady and supportive, and your inside hand elastic, softly giving and taking. (If you were to pull, he'd raise his head, tense, and probably bulge his outside shoulder.)

B. As you approach the beginning of the first loop (see diagram, opposite page), look right around the curving track, turning your upper body so your right shoulder is slightly behind your left. Drop your weight into your right heel without tilting, and show your horse where you want him to go by bending him along the track with the very least amount of inside rein you can use. Avoid the temptation to lean into the new direction, instead staying centered and balanced above your horse.

C. As you approach the midpoint of the S, ride a straight line for a few strides, then prepare to change your bend from right to left. First look left and visualize the track. Then turn your upper body so your left shoulder is slightly behind your right. Smoothly bring your right leg a bit behind the girth and your left leg into the girth.

D. Take a light feel on the new outside rein with your right hand, and show your horse the way to the new bend by guiding him to the left. Change your posting

SOME POINTERS AND GROUND RULES:

➤ **Check him out.** No exercise can teach your horse to do quiet flying changes if he's physically incapable of them, so watch him during turnout to make sure he swaps leads on his own. If he never does, or if you're already having trouble teaching him, ask your veterinarian to check him over.

➤ **Think big.** Work in as large an area as possible, for two reasons: Your counter-canter figures will be more doable, and your horse will be less liable to orient himself in terms of the wrong lead—a major cue for panic. An open field is ideal, but an arena no smaller than 150 by 300 feet will work as well.

➤ **Go mild.** Use a mild snaffle bit and a regular bridle. I'm not a fan of standing martingales, but you may need one for this work if your horse throws his head.

➤ **Make it stick.** An inexpensive dressage whip (in what will be the inside hand of your new lead) works better than a stick, because you can lightly touch him without the big, tension-creating punishment of bridging your reins and reaching down to make contact.

➤ **Say thanks.** When your horse is successful, try reinforcing him with a treat, such as an equine cookie, carrots, or sugar cubes (carried in a pocket). After each clean change, canter a half-circle on the new lead, then stop your horse, reach forward and pop a treat into his mouth to say "thanks."

➤ **Avoid drilling him.** Do all exercises in both directions. Repeat each step enough times during a session that your horse understands what you want, but don't drill him to the point where he becomes bored or upset. And stay with each step until you feel it's solid, no matter how many sessions that takes.

➤ **Be patient.** Fixing flying changes is a ticklish business. This program will work only if you undertake it

(Continued)

with quiet, reassuring riding and a patient mindset. Keeping your horse relaxed and trusting is critical to achieving the desired proficiencies. Any time he starts to get upset, you're either asking too much or going too fast. Go back, do more work on the earlier exercises, and remind yourself that even though fluid flying changes are your goal, they're not your only goal. The process itself must be enjoyable for horse and rider.

➤ **Prevent high anxiety.** If your horse is already so upset by lead changes that he speeds up or gets tense and loses straightness any time he changes direction, put the pattern on hold and work on my "Cure For High Anxiety," page 66. Take a week, three months, or whatever time you need to get him completely relaxed and ho-hum about changes of direction before you tackle changes of lead.

➤ **Keep it real.** If nerves, poor balance, impatience, or lack of body control cause you to tense, hang on the reins, or bounce on your horse's back, you can't help him through this program. You'll serve your partnership better by engaging a capable, patient professional to do it for you.

diagonal as he flows smoothly (without speeding up, slowing down, or falling in or out on the track) from right to left.

E. Continue on, then practice the figure in both directions until you feel confident and comfortable with it. (If this takes days—or weeks—that's fine!)

Now, Canter the S-Shape

When you're ready to canter the exercise (starting with a right-to-left lead change):

1. Sit in a secure, modified, two-point position (your breeches just off the saddle), with your outside (left) leg slightly behind the girth and your inside (right) leg firmly at the girth. Move your right hand forward until there's a slight loop in the rein, and ask your horse to step forward into a steady, relaxed, controlled, three-beat right-lead canter on a big (at least 60-foot) circle. Bring your right hand back until you have equal contact with both reins. But, just as at the trot, make your outside hand steady and supportive, and your inside hand elastic.

When you feel your horse is steady and balanced (he stays on your outside rein for a few strides when you move your right hand forward, without changing rhythm),

begin the first loop of your S, just as you did at the trot. Use your eyes first, upper body next, and a close/soften/close/soften on the inside rein to bend him on the track.

2. As you approach the midpoint of the S, straighten your horse for a stride or two, then start the change of bend from right to left by looking around the new track to the left. Slightly turn your upper body until your left shoulder is a little behind your right. Bring your left leg onto the girth to keep your horse from falling in on the new curve, and your right leg slightly behind the girth. Let your left hand—which up to now has maintained a fairly steady, consistent feel on the outside rein—become as light and giving as you can possibly make it while still guiding him into the new left bend. And let your right hand assume the equally light but steady feel of the outside rein.

3. What will happen? A flying change, we hope, because your horse should simply make himself comfortable on the left bend by switching to his left lead. If he does a clean flying change without changing

speed, continue cantering on the second loop, stay quiet, and don't grab or restrict him. Put both hands forward and make a loop in the reins to reward him for a couple of strides, then quietly feel his mouth again. (If he doesn't change leads, see "Troubleshooting Tips," below.)

Practice three times each way. Then, depending on the results you get and your horse's temperament, use your judgment to determine if you should practice again in your next session. With lead changes, less is better than more, practice wise. You want your horse to stay relaxed about the changes. If you're unsure about how often to practice, consult with a reputable trainer.

As you and your horse gain confidence with the exercise, gradually make the S-shape more shallow, using less bending preparation, until your horse can change on a straight line—your end goal. (If he loses ground, go back to the S shape.)

Don't rush. Set yourself up for success. Wait until your changes are solid in both directions on the S before going onto more challenging locations, such as on the diagonal and after fences.

If your horse runs through the S, getting more nervous and anxious the longer you do it, that's a big red light. Go back to the anxiety-easing exercise on page 66, or back off completely until you can get some professional help.

Troubleshooting Tips

I would love at this point for your horse to do a clean flying change. However, if he doesn't, or does but is panicked about it, use the following troubleshooting tips:

➤ **He speeds up:** Rushing through the change may mean you came on a little strong when you changed your leg position. Make a quiet downward transition to the trot, steer back around to the right, and ride a quiet trot circle to relax and reassure him. Then pick up the canter and try the S shape again. But, be quieter and more subtle with your leg aids.

➤ **He changes in front, but not behind:** Sit up, take an even, steady feel on both reins, and put a little pressure on his mouth, as if you're getting ready for a trot transition. (Don't forget to support it with slightly increased leg pressure.) That will help him balance, redistribute his weight, and "catch" the new left lead behind.

➤ **He ignores your aids:** If he doesn't appear to respond to the new bend at all, just cantering quietly and rhythmically on, touch him with your dressage whip behind your left leg, without breaking your wrist, to remind him that he can step forward with the new inside left hind. (We're always told to use the outside leg to ask for the change, but to me it's the inside hind leg that fails to step under.)

A CURE FOR HIGH ANXIETY

Here's how to reduce tension in your ultra-anxious horse. Ride a shallow serpentine pattern along the rail, in which you counter-canter the mild changes of direction—referring back to Lesson 4—to show him that a change of direction doesn't necessarily forecast a flying lead change.

As you counter-canter through the serpentine, anytime you feel him speed up, slow down, tense, lean, or otherwise display anxiety, smoothly turn him in the direction of the lead you're on, circle, then return to the rail and try again.

The key is for you to stay calm, and quiet. That way, every time he says, "EEEEEK, it's a lead change!" you'll calmly respond with "No, it isn't—it's just another canter stride," until you can keep him cantering softly on either lead, with a variety of direction changes, whenever you go in the ring. Only at that point should you resume the lead-change exercise in this chapter.

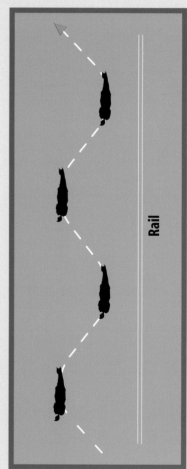

High-Anxiety Cure

If your horse gets explosive about his lead changes, this serpentine, counter-canter exercise can help.

Let's Jump!

BEFORE WE TACKLE LINES AND A COURSE, REVIEW YOUR
JUMPING BASICS—AND BUILD ON YOUR CONFIDENCE—
WITH THESE THREE SIMPLE EXERCISES.

Are you ready to graduate from poles on the ground to real jumps? I'll bet you are. So you can focus on improving your jumping skills—and confidence—these first fences will be small (mostly crossrails and very low verticals). This will lessen your anxiety over the consequences of a mistake. And throughout most of this lesson, the distances between fences will be predetermined, so you won't have to worry about seeing a distance for now.

Instead, you can relax and focus on maintaining rhythm, balance, and your position, both over and between the fences. (More about that below.)

WHAT YOU'LL NEED:

➤ A level work area with good footing, large enough to accommodate a multi-jump gymnastic.
➤ Enough standards, poles, and cups to create a trot-pole-to-two-jump gymnastic. (See diagrams in this lesson.)
➤ Two cones or standards (with cups removed or facing outward, for safety), for use as markers.

A FEW BASIC POINTERS TO KEEP IN MIND:

➤ **Balance:** Most jumping problems are balance problems, and most begin with the rider: You're thinking so much about the jump you forget about yourself. In this lesson, you'll get to build on your jumping skills from jumps you don't have to think about. The repetitive efforts and set distances will give you practice maintaining your balance, as well as your horse's.

➤ **Position:** You'll jump in two-point position, rising into it two strides before the first fence. Assuming the position early will help build your strength and prevent you from making a big move in front of the jump. In short, you'll learn to wait and let the jump come to you.

➤ **Hands:** You'll start this lesson with a *crest release*, in which you'll plant your hands on your horse's crest from takeoff to landing. That way, you'll become accustomed to the jumping effort without interfering with your horse's head and neck. The crest release, which you'll assume about five feet from the fence, also helps you stabilize your position.

Before you go on to single fences in our future lessons, which require extra control, you can make the transition to a *following*, or out-of-hand release, in which your hands follow your horse's head from take-off to landing, with your reins in a direct line from your elbows to your horse's mouth.

➤ **Rhythm:** Maintaining the steady rhythm and balance of your horse's pace will be your first priority throughout these exercises. As long as his stride is rhythmic and balanced, you'll have a comfortable jumping effort even if the distance isn't perfect, because your horse will make his own adjustments to get you over safely. Later, as your technique and eye improve, you'll find it easy to lengthen or shorten a few inches in each stride from a steady, balanced pace.

➤ **Confidence:** All the exercises in my program are designed to build confidence, but work best if you take active control of your thinking. If you're nervous about jumping, admit it to yourself and take positive steps to deal with it before you approach a fence. Train yourself to slow down, take a deep breath, and regroup at the first twinge of fear. Make yourself run through your position checklist, check your horse's balance and pace, and take it easy. If you take back at the fence, or you run at it and ask him to stand way off—both typical reactions of nervous riders—you'll impair his balance. Do either often and you'll also impair both his form and his confidence.

EXERCISE 1:
"X" WITH A TROT RAIL

In this exercise, striding and takeoff spots are totally predictable—after the pole your horse will take one step with each front foot and then pop over the cross-rail—so you're free to concentrate on learning or refreshing the principles of jumping.

Set up an 18-inch crossrail with a ground rail; lay a pole on the ground 7 feet in front of it. Place two markers (such as cones or standards) 15 feet before the pole to flank your approach. (See diagram, at right.)

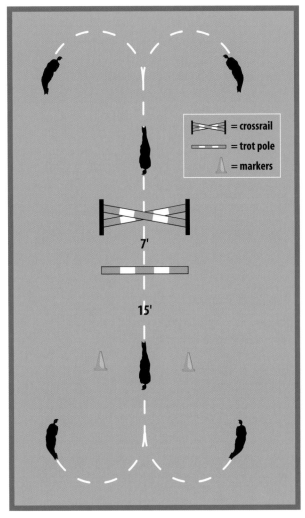

Exercise 1: "X" With a Trot Rail

1. Before you begin, pick a focal point about 40 feet beyond the center of the jump, to help you keep your eyes up, which will also help maintain your balance. Establish an active, rhythmic posting trot and approach on a straight track that aims your horse at the center of the crossrail; look at the crossrail as you approach. Rise into two-point position when you reach the markers.

2. Raise your eyes to your focal point—the jump will stay in your peripheral vision—and give a crest release, as shown.

TROUBLESHOOTING

Analyze any problem you may have had, so that you can avoid it next time. For instance:

1A. Your horse rushes the pole/crossrail. If your horse quickens as he canters the pole and crossrail, lay a pole on the ground to the right or left of the the crossrail, as shown in the photo at right. Begin your approach as if you were going to jump the crossrail, but gradually change the track, heading off to the single pole instead, keeping a soft feel of your horse's mouth.

Repeat the single pole until your horse relaxes and stops anticipating, then try the pole and crossrail again. Alternate between the two, keeping a soft feel until takeoff and giving a slightly more generous release over the crossrail than over the pole. Don't let your upper body move forward or your legs grab, both of which would inadvertently send him "go!" signals, which is the opposite of your goal.

1B. You look down. If you had trouble staying in position in the air, you may have forgotten to look up when you reached the pole. Have your helper stand about 40 feet beyond the center of the crossrail, with an arm raised above her head; ask her to hold up a different number of fingers each time you approach. As you reach the pole, look at your helper and tell her how many fingers she's holding up. Not only will your head stay up, but your concentration on counting fingers will distract you from worrying about your fence and produce a better jumping effort.

1C. You fell forward or backward. If you slumped forward over your horse's neck or fell back in the saddle in the landing, your balance needs work. Practice holding two-point over a single pole on the ground, as shown at right. Then try the crossrail exercise again, but assume the two-point position earlier and remind yourself several times to put weight in your heels. Grab mane if necessary, and land into your heels. If you concentrate on what's happening with your position at every stride, you'll soon identify and correct your weak spot, as well as build strength and confidence.

3. As your horse passes over the pole, weight your heels a little more forcefully; you don't have to do anything with your upper body. His forehand will automatically close your hip angle over the upcoming jump.

4. As your horse canters or pops over the jump, think, "Land into my legs," so you absorb the shock of landing in your ankles and heels. (Your crest release will support your upper body.)

5. Most horses land in a canter from a trot jump. If yours doesn't, send him forward immediately so he gets used to the idea of landing in a canter; on a line of fences, he'll need to maintain a canter to meet his next jump properly.

6. Maintain your two-point position for three or four more canter strides before bringing your horse back to a walk. If he's sluggish, close your legs, sit up, and take a feel of his mouth to revive his energy.

When you feel comfortable with takeoff, jump, and landing, you're ready to move on—but don't hurry. If you need more practice on the exercise, set up another pole-crossrail combination elsewhere in your ring; vary your work location to keep from souring your horse. (And, avoid practicing this or *any* jumping exercise for more than 15 or 20 minutes.)

After initially stopping on a straight line, practice continuing a turn while maintaining the quality of the canter—just as you'll have to do when we start jumping courses.

EXERCISE 2:
ADD A SECOND CROSSRAIL

If you're an anxious rider, you likely jump fences hunched over your hands, throwing your weight over your horse's forehand, and disturbing his balance. In other words, you do too much, rather than being relaxed and still.

This exercise, which calls for a second crossrail 18

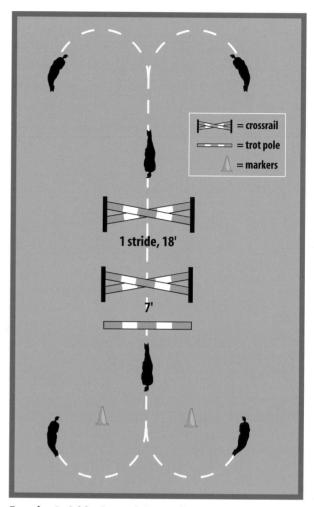

Exercise 2: Add a Second Crossrail

feet from the first one, reinforces the habit of doing nothing once you've prepared for a fence. (See diagram above.) The pole sets up your takeoff for the first jump; and 18 feet allows your horse one canter stride before the second. You'll have no reason to be nervous, because you're set up to succeed. All you have to do is maintain your position.

7. Ride the first part of the exercise as before. When your horse lands from the first crossrail…

8. …maintain your two-point position and your crest release for the single stride…

9. …and over the second crossrail. Then stay in that position through the landing and for several strides

TROUBLESHOOTING II

You may find you're having one of these typical problems with this exercise:

2A. You pop up between fences. You come back with your upper body and pick up your hands from your horse's neck between crossrails, as shown. Many riders worry their horses will take evasive action if they maintain a forward position between fences, so they come back almost involuntarily. Braid a section of mane a few inches up your horse's neck, where your hands will rest in a crest release. As you move your hands forward at the pole, hold the braid between the thumb and forefinger of your right hand and place your left hand next to it.

2B. You make a big move with your upper body between crossrails. This hurrying effort only unsettles your horse. (Just look at this horse's expression—he's mad!) To distract yourself from the urge to do it, ask your helper to hold up her hand again. Focus on her fingers and your position. Remember, the two fences are spaced perfectly for one comfortable canter stride, even if your horse is a little long-strided or short-strided.

2C. You feel your horse drifting between the crossrails. To keep him straight, lay two painted rails—not plain ones, which he might not see well—parallel to your track, forming a chute as wide as your jumps. Be sure to approach along a straight path that brings you to the center of the first crossrail.

Use a light opening rein on the side away from the drift, and soften your other hand to let your horse respond to the correction. Then move both hands into the crest release and let the guidepoles keep him straight for the rest of the exercise. (If he continues to drift, you can roll them a few feet closer together, to further encourage the "straight" message.) Once he's moving forward to his fences in a rhythmic, balanced stride, most of his drifting problems will disappear.

When you're doing this exercise correctly, the angle of your back and the position of your hands will stay the same over both jumps, and your horse will maintain an even pace throughout. If he quickens or slows, spend more time establishing pace before you approach the first crossrail, then monitor your position during the exercise to be sure you aren't causing the problem.

beyond the second jump, before bringing him back to a walk. Holding your position for this extended period develops your security, which, in turn, helps you maintain your horse's balance. (If he gets quick, take a soft feel as you land from the first jump and give again for the second, but stay in two-point so your seat doesn't inadvertently drive him forward.)

EXERCISE 3:
GRADUATE TO A VERTICAL

Make the second crossrail into a 2-foot vertical. (See diagram at right.) Striding and takeoff are still totally predictable; the small additional height gives a feeling of a little extra thrust—but not so much that you need to change your technique or experience any concern.

10. When your horse rounds his back over this slightly higher jump, you may feel him push your weight up-

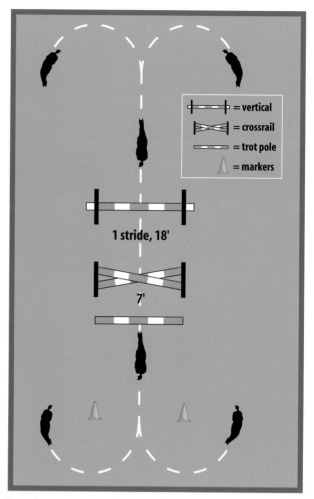

Exercise 3: Graduate to a Vertical

ward, so that it rests more on the balls of your feet than in your heels. If you maintain your position (you can use a following release, as shown, or stick with the crest release, if that's more comfortable), a split second later your weight will sink back into your heels and you'll land securely, ready to regroup in the control stride.

11. But if you're trying too hard and gripping with your ankles instead of sinking your weight into your heels, you'll feel your legs slip back as you go over the vertical. Remind yourself to relax, step into your heels, and look up. Concentrate on your focal point and you'll find your position improves automatically.

When you feel comfortable with these three exercises, you're ready to graduate to Lesson 8: Related Distances.

Related Distances

BY ADDING RELATED DISTANCES IN THESE THREE GYMNASTIC
EXERCISES, YOU'LL BUILD ON YOUR SENSE OF YOUR
HORSE'S STRIDE IN RELATION TO A FENCE, WHICH WILL
PREPARE YOU FOR CANTERING A SINGLE FENCE.

We'll now build on the jumping (and confidence) basics you learned in Lesson 7, by adding a third and fourth element to that lesson's two-jump gymnastic exercise. This will help you develop the strength and flexibility needed to maintain your jumping position for a longer period of time, which will help when we begin course work later. It'll also develop a sense of your horse's stride in relation to a fence.

The distance from the second to the third element will allow for one normal canter stride between low fences. When you're comfortable, you'll add a fourth element five strides away, which will help improve your eye (and confidence!) riding to a single fence.

Whatever combination of crossrails and verticals you choose, the distance works comfortably and gives very predictable striding. Your horse will trot in and over the first crossrail, take one canter stride, jump the center element, land, take one more stride, and jump out.

You'll have three opportunities to practice your jumping form without worrying about the jumps. (Meanwhile, this gymnastic will be improving your horse's form, making him a more comfortable ride—and you more secure in your position.)

WHAT YOU'LL NEED:

➤ A level work area with good footing, large enough to accommodate a multi-jump gymnastic.

➤ Enough standards and poles to set up a gymnastic that will eventually contain a trot pole, three crossrails or verticals, and an oxer.

➤ Cones or standards (cups removed, for safety), for use as markers.

EXERCISE 1:
ADD A THIRD ELEMENT

Turn to page 74 to see the two-element gymnastic set-up there. Here, you'll add a third element, 21 feet (one stride) from the second one. (See diagram, page 77.) If you feel completely comfortable with the crossrail-to-vertical combination, add a second low (2-foot) vertical. Otherwise, add a crossrail; you can drop the second element back to a crossrail, too.

Review Lesson 7, then use the same approach to this gymnastic. Practice the habit of looking ahead. Pick a distant focal point as you approach the gymnastic and begin looking at it as soon as you've lined your horse up with the first crossrail.

As you did in Lesson 7, move into the two-point, and move your hands into a crest release, several strides from the ground pole (keep looking up!); you'll maintain that position until you land from the last fence.

1. Keep your weight in your heels and your eyes up over the second jump. As you land, focus on maintaining your position, your horse's rhythm, and keeping your eyes on the third jump.

> If your horse tends to drift between jumps, you can straighten him using ground poles, so you don't have to move your hands. For how to do it, see Lesson 7: Troubleshooting II, page 73.
>
> *TIP*

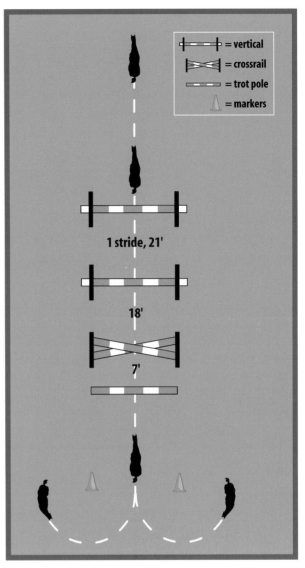

Exercise 1: Add a Third Element

Legend:
- ⊢╌╌╌⊣ = vertical
- ⋈ = crossrail
- ▬╌╌▬ = trot pole
- △ = markers

1 stride, 21'

18'

7'

2. Then return your gaze to the focal point and concentrate on the feel of that single stride…

3. … and the takeoff spot over the third fence. Don't try to influence what's happening; just allow yourself to be aware of it. Land with your weight in your heels, and canter straight ahead for several strides as you did in Lesson 7, then reward your horse and repeat. When you can maintain your position from the pole to the last fence of a crossrail-vertical-vertical combination, you're ready to move on.

EXERCISE 2:
LET'S JUMP AN OXER

Turn the final vertical into an oxer by putting another 2-foot vertical 2 feet beyond it. (See diagram at right.) The distance remains the same, so your striding and take-off spot are still predictable. You're free to concentrate on maintaining your position over the extra width.

    (If the idea of jumping an oxer at this point makes you nervous, proceed directly to the next exercise. But if you're secure over the gymnastic with two verticals, you'll find the wider fence really isn't a problem.)

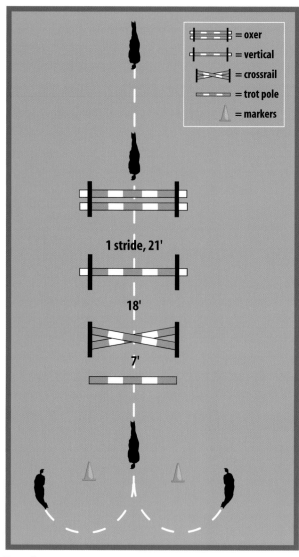

Exercise 2: Let's Jump an Oxer

4. To ensure you don't fall back or forward, step a little deeper into your heels as you ride the stride to the oxer. If you feel you might drop back, especially with a horse that jumps up rather than across his fences, hold the mane, to avoid inadvertently bumping your horse in the mouth.

5. This oxer is low and not very wide (your horse may simply canter over it, as this horse is doing here). Nonetheless, you'll feel a little more thrust as your horse stays in the air a bit longer and rounds his back a bit more over the spread. Avoid changing your position; his effort will close the angle of your two-point, just as it does over verticals.

6. When you land, be sure to sink your weight into your legs and heels, and to maintain your crest release to avoid interfering with your horse's balance. Canter away from the jump for several strides, then reward him (give yourself a pat on the back, too), and repeat.

EXERCISE 3:
ADD A "SINGLE" FENCE

In this exercise, you'll add a single 2-foot vertical five easy strides from the gymnastic, which will help you recognize where you are in relation to a single fence. (See diagram at right.) Since you know the distance will work out, you can concentrate on memorizing what you see, stride for stride, as you approach the fence. The exercise also teaches mental discipline. It's hard to sit still and concentrate on holding your balanced stride together when you don't "see" anything, distance-wise. But that's the safest way to approach a fence.

If you kick on or pull back when you don't see a take-off spot, you could be asking your horse to stand way off or chip into the fence. If, however, you simply sit up and maintain his rhythm, focusing on your focal point—rather than the fence—if you don't see a distance, he'll be in sufficient balance to make his own adjustment by "patting the ground." The worst fence you'll have is one that's a little too short.

You can make this single fence by moving the gymnastic's third element, or by keeping the gymnastic intact and adding a new fence, so you have four in all. Using a 3-foot step, walk off 22 strides beyond the gymnastic's last element, plus 2 feet (a total of 68 feet). Place the new fence there. With your boot heel, draw a line in the dirt about 2 feet

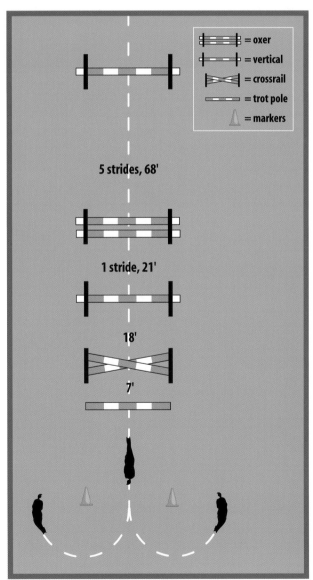

Exercise 3: Add a "Single" Fence

in front of the jump; this will be the takeoff point you'll aim for.

Your horse may not hit that line in the dirt with his feet every time, but he'll be within his safety margin as long as you keep your position and avoid the big moves that require last-second adjustments. Don't sink back toward three-point position to shorten or lean forward to lengthen. Adjusting the relationship of your hands and legs will do the job safely. And any time you're not sure what adjustment you need to make, stay quiet and let your horse do it. He'll take care of himself—and you.

7. Ride the first part of the exercise as you have been. As your horse takes the control stride away from the gymnastic, maintain a comfortable, active canter. Stay in your two-point position and look at the single fence as you count, "One…two …three …."

8. Don't struggle to "see" anything. Continue to focus on the fence until stride three; then switch to your focal point but continue to be aware of where you are in relation to the obstacle. Hold the balanced stride…

9. …and jump. Canter straight for five or six strides, then circle, bring your horse to a trot, and repeat the exercise. When you've ridden the line several times, start trying to see a connection between the numbers you say and the distance you see.

You probably won't see anything for the first two strides, but when your horse arrives at or near the line in the dirt, you'll feel the familiar takeoff distance that he uses over the gymnastic. Gradually you'll begin to feel the relationship of stride to distance on stride four, then on three.

Each time you say "three," look at the fence and tell yourself, "That's what two strides out should look like." Then immediately look back at your focal point. When you automatically know you're two strides from the fence, your "eye" is beginning to develop.

10. Once you can recognize that you're three strides in front of the fence, you can safely begin adjusting your horse's stride.

Start with the way he lands from the gymnastic: If it's a little slower than his active pace, you know the five-stride distance is going to ride a little more forward. To reach the single fence comfortably, you'll have to lengthen his stride a little, as this rider is doing here. You don't have to change position to lengthen the few inches you need. Just ask for a canter one notch above your horse's normal pace in the first

TROUBLESHOOTING TIPS

➤ **Think, before you adjust.** Even if you sense where you are in relation to the "single" jump, don't adjust your horse's stride unless you're *absolutely* sure you'll make the distance work out better. Instead, concentrate on holding the balance and rhythm.

➤ **Remember your mantra: It's only flatwork....** If your horse's pace quickens or slows, tell yourself, "It's just flatwork," and correct as you would if there were no jump ahead.

➤ **Keep it quiet.** Discipline yourself to pass up any forward distances you see, which could make your horse anxious. Instead, when a correction is necessary, stay relaxed and think, "Pull together and add a stride." Close your fingers on the reins, maintain rhythm with your leg, and let your horse compress his stride so he meets the fence off a short one.

➤ **Feel it.** If you think he isn't shortening enough, and you're going to meet the fence too close, make yourself smoothly increase your feel a little and sit still. Don't give in to your natural urge to jerk him in the mouth and back him off, which would break up his balance and rhythm. Stay relaxed and hold.

At worst he'll take off a little short, maybe knocking down the fence—a safer option than a fast canter leading to a long distance, which could land him in the middle of the jump. Holding a steady, quiet pace is a good decision for your horse if he tends to anticipate. Stay relaxed and he'll learn to do the same.

➤ **Do a position check.** If your horse is steady on the flat but gets quick and strong when he jumps, check yourself. You may be anticipating with your legs or hanging on his mouth. If you're satisfied that you're not at fault, relax him by alternating fences with poles on the ground.

three strides. Then stay quiet for the final two. You'll reach the fence comfortably.

11. If you land from the gymnastic a little quick, close your fingers in the control stride. As you feel the pace resume its normal activity and length, soften your feel and let the fence come up comfortably.

12. Before you advance to the next lesson, ask your helper to watch the takeoff line and tell you how close you're coming to it. If your horse's feet consistently touch the line or come within 6 to 8 inches of it, you're ready to move on.

If you consistently go beyond the line, you may be shortening too much or too little. Analyze your performance (your helper can help) and decide which correction you need to make. (See "Troubleshooting Tips," page 81.)

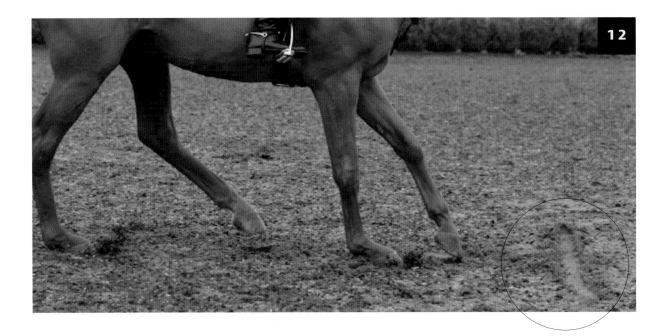

Fear-Free Single Fences

USE THIS GREAT EXERCISE FOR TAKING THE FEAR OUT OF
JUMPING SINGLE FENCES. IT'LL ALSO HELP DEVELOP
YOUR EYE FOR A DISTANCE.

Up to now, you've been jumping gymnastics and related distances, meaning you've been set up to jump fences after a predetermined number of strides. Doing so enabled you to relax and focus on yourself and your horse, thus building confidence. You've also developed a feel for the correct takeoff spot in front of a "single" fence, thanks to Lesson 8.

In this lesson, you'll learn to jump a single fence, perfectly out of stride—just as you'd do on a hunter or jumper course. But rather than simply pointing your horse at a lone fence in the distance, I'm going to make it easy for you, to further build on your confidence.

You'll start by jumping from big canter circles that alternate over tiny obstacles. Doing so will allow you to relax and notice how easily your horse does the exercise. As the diagram below shows, it's really simple. You start with a circle that goes over a pole on the ground; then you add a circle over a flowerbox beside the pole, then a circle over a small crossrail or vertical (your choice). It's not really a progression; you circle alternately among the three low obstacles.

The almost mesmerizing repetition and the simplicity of the obstacles are what make this exercise work. In the ring, many people are too nervous to think, so they have no technique. They see the jump, know they're supposed to do it, then somehow they're on the other side and all they know is how relieved they are.

But going over these tiny obstacles again and again lets you relax and become aware of what's happening beneath you: your horse's rhythm, the track he's following, his straightness—the tools that produce a good jump.

WHAT YOU'LL NEED:

➤ A work area with good footing and room for a comfortably large canter circle (about 60-foot in diameter at the minimum).

➤ A ground pole.

➤ Two 6-foot flowerboxes.

➤ Two standards and three (for a vertical) or four (for a crossrail) rails; a longe line and longe whip.

Circles of Confidence

Place a pole on the ground across the track. In line with the pole, as the diagram at right shows, put a couple of 6-foot flowerboxes end to end (or a railroad tie or log). Just beyond the flowerboxes, set a very low jump with ground lines on both sides.

Begin by longeing your horse over the two lowest obstacles (but only if you both are proficient in the art of longeing; if not, skip to the riding part of this exercise). Why? So you can watch him doing the exercise on his own—and see how easily he does it. Tack him

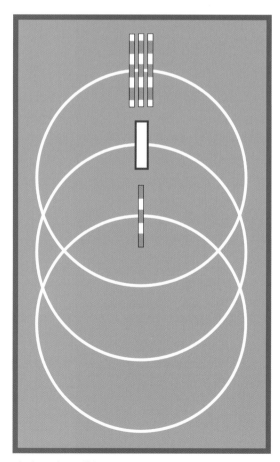

Circles of Confidence

up in a saddle and bridle, but run up the stirrups so they won't bang on his sides, and loop your reins under the stirrups to keep them from flopping.

Get him going on the longe in a nice rhythmic working canter, on whichever lead is easier for him, and guide him so he goes over the center of the pole. Watch and you'll see that all he needs to meet the pole comfortably is to be on track to its center in a rhythmic stride, with freedom to use his head and neck.

When he's meeting the pole comfortably every time, take a few steps toward the flowerbox so you can longe him over its center. The tiny additional height may let you see more easily whether he's meeting the flowerbox at a perfect takeoff spot, or 6 inches long, or 6 inches short.

More importantly, you'll also see that he adjusts on his own to make it work, without changing his rhythm. Watch how comfortably he meets it. He'll do the same when you start riding him over these obstacles, as long as you maintain his rhythm and track.

When he's longeing smoothly over the pole and flowerbox, begin the under-saddle part of the exercise. Mount up, then walk and trot for a few minutes to warm yourself up.

1. Now establish that same rhythmic canter your horse had on the longe, on his "easy" lead, and maintain it around the circle. (For more info, see "Circle Smarts," page 87.)

2. Be peripherally aware that the pole is there, but don't try to do anything about it—keep your eyes up and on a focal point ahead. Let him find the distance on his own—you've seen that he can.

4. When you're comfortably cantering over the pole, adjust your circle to canter over the flowerbox. Do that a couple of times, then circle over the pole again. Then alternate between the two. If you can, recruit a friend to help, by calling out, "Pole, flowerbox, flowerbox again, pole...."

Keep your position the same, so that if I blocked out my view of the horse and just watched you, I couldn't tell whether you were going over the pole or the flowerbox.

3. If he goes long or steps all over the pole, you're probably leaning forward as this rider is here, or otherwise interfering. Instead, sit up, sit still, and concentrate on keeping the rhythm, maintaining the lead, and letting your horse do the rest while you take note of how you're meeting the pole.

5. When you're comfortable with the flowerbox, move your circle to go over your little jump in that same rhythmic canter. Do that a couple of times; then do the pole—it'll be easier than ever—and the flowerbox.

Coming back repeatedly to the simplest version of the exercise is key to making it work. Continue repeating and alternating, solidifying that rhythmic feeling and storing it in your memory.

For variety, you can make the circle larger or smaller. When you feel really solid on your horse's easier lead, repeat the whole process on the harder lead. Keep coming back to the pole until your inner self says you don't need to any more.

With time and repetition, you'll begin to develop an "eye" and a sense of whether you're going to be a little long or a little tight. Then—calmly and deliberately, your fear of jumping single fences gone—you'll learn to influence your horse's canter to adjust for the distance. (I'll give you specifics for how to do so in Lesson 11: Adjustability, page 99.)

If your horse should fall in or out of the circle, or speed up or slow down, refer back to Lesson 5: Pole Power, "Cantering Poles On A Circle," for trouble-shooting tips.

CIRCLE SMARTS

As you guide your horse around the single-fence circle exercise, keep these tips in mind, to maximize success (and confidence-building).

➤ **Create.** Use the early third of the circle to create your horse's rhythm and pace. (See diagram below.)

➤ **Maintain.** Sit still and maintain that rhythm for the second third, which will be your approach to the pole, flowerbox, or jump.

➤ **Repair.** And use the early part of the final third, immediately after the obstacle, to repair any alterations to your horse's rhythm or stride.

As you can see, the point is to make any changes *early* in the circle, then to sit still and simply maintain your horse's rhythm and balance as you approach the obstacle.

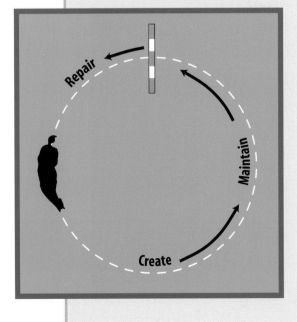

Learning Your Lines

IMPROVE YOUR EYE—AND YOUR CONFIDENCE—
BY LEARNING TO JUMP INTO AND OUT OF LINES.

With this lesson, you're going to assume a new level of responsibility: adjusting your horse's stride so he meets his fences smoothly. Up to now you've relied on your insurance plan: You made sure your position was right, you concentrated on keeping your horse's stride balanced and rhythmic, and his pace and track correct, and you let him find a safe distance to his fences.

Now, using a six-stride line of two low jumps, you'll work on meeting each fence at the same distance—and on making subtle, effective adjustments early, so the closer you come to the fence, the less you have to do. This is key: Whatever the height of the fences you face in the future, you'll find the principles you learn here will apply.

In this exercise, for instance, you have a related distance—a normal six-stride line—in which the way you ride the first jump will affect the way you meet the second. To make the whole line appear as smooth as possible, you want to meet the first fence out of a normal stride.

If you see an abnormally long distance to that fence, one that requires a lot of leg, your adjustment is going to be very obvious because it will be out of context with the rest of the line. Since your horse will jump into the line with too much pace and stride, you'll also need to make another obvious adjustment to the second fence. In addition, your chasing him will encourage him to rush his fences, so he'll jump each line in increasingly poor balance and rhythm; he'll also jump flat. That's why this exercise is so key: It'll help you make each fence look the same, which will make the line appear to flow smoothly and effortlessly. It's more fun to ride that way, and more pleasing for a judge to look at.

To be sure you're fully prepared to learn your lines, fulfill the requirements in the "Take-Stock Checklist" on page 91. Until you do, you'd risk undoing all the good confidence-building work we've done up to this point.

WHAT YOU'LL NEED:

➤ A flat, level work area with good footing, and room for a six-stride line.

➤ Enough standards and poles to set up two fences for the line.

Set Up for a Six-Stride Line

Set up two, 2-foot jumps 82 feet apart. (*NOTE:* Later, if you raise your jumps to 3 feet, add 2 feet to the line to give yourself a 4-foot takeoff and landing. If your horse is short- or long-strided, adjust these distances by a foot or two so they ride normally for him. See "Determining Stride Length," page 93.) Use rails if solid jumps make you nervous. You're not trying to challenge yourself here; you're setting up another

TIP

On any lines or course you jump, your ability to discipline your thoughts is basic to your success. Don't let yourself worry about whether you'll do your job. Instead, focus on helping your horse do his job—to jump in the best form he can.

Whenever you catch your nerves taking over, deliberately switch your thoughts to a positive track. For example, instead of letting yourself think, "Oh, I'm so scared of that oxer," tell yourself, "Let's see. The line from the vertical to the oxer rides in a steady six, so I have to establish that pace before I turn to the first fence, and I must remember to shorten in my control stride."

Keep yourself so tuned in to what your horse is doing, stride for stride, that nervousness becomes a luxury you can't afford. Also, even when you're not in the tack, visualize yourself riding the lines correctly. The brain is a powerful tool; that vision will become a reality when you ride.

controlled situation in which you can learn the principles that apply for any line of fences.

For your balancing and organizing "homework," make sure that you have at least a six-stride straight approach before your first fence, and a six-stride straightaway after your second. If your ring is a little

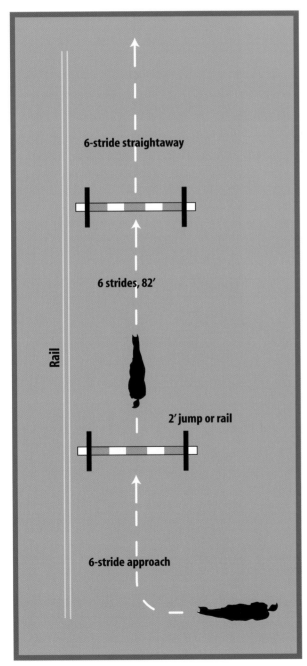

6-stride straightaway

6 strides, 82'

Rail

2' jump or rail

6-stride approach

Six-Stride Line

Remember: You never need to advance to more demanding work until you're totally secure in the work you're doing, so you keep building your confidence (the point of this book) rather than eroding it.

With that in mind, and because learning to ride lines is a prelude to our upcoming course work, make certain you can check off all the following boxes before you tackle this lesson. If you can't, keep on with the previous lesson's exercises until you do.

❏ You have 90-percent control of all gaits on the flat. Perfect control isn't a realistic goal; your horse is an animal, not a robot. But you should feel that his response to your leg and hand aids is consistent and accurate, so you can move him deeper into a corner, bring him onto a smaller circle, or adjust the length of his stride at least nine times out of 10.

❏ You feel totally comfortable in two-point and three-point positions at all three gaits—and especially at your jumping pace—and can maintain your balance, your horse's balance, and his rhythm from those positions.

❏ You're able to recognize and create the correct jumping pace. You feel your horse carrying himself as he works energetically from his hindquarters, each hind leg tracking under his body with a powerful movement. With each stride you should feel he's "in front of your leg," pushing—almost as if he were going through deep sand or water—with a self-starting energy that doesn't need frequent revivals from you.

❏ You feel comfortable with all the gymnastic exercises in previous lessons, so you can stay relaxed while consistently maintaining your horse's balance and controlling his pace.

❏ When you're approaching a fence, your instinctive reaction is to relax, hold the stride together, and let your horse set himself up for a comfortable takeoff spot. This is your ticket to a successful jump—and your insurance against a bad one, even when the unexpected happens.

❏ You have enough of an eye to recognize when you're three strides in front of the fence and whether the distance is going to be right or wrong.

short, you may be able to give yourself enough room by setting up your line on a diagonal; otherwise, move the exercise out to a level field.

You'll need the room to evaluate your pace, balance, and rhythm before cantering out of a turn to navigate the line, and to rebalance before cantering around the far end of the ring after your second fence.

Even though you'll only be jumping a single line, you want to establish the habit of reorganizing immediately at the end of it *now*, so you don't find your horse becoming increasingly strung-out and hard to balance with every line when you jump a course.

Let's Ride!

1. Warm up your horse (see Lesson 13: Course-Work Warm-Up) and briefly review Lesson 9, to prepare him for work over fences. When you're both confident and relaxed, pick up a canter at the end of your ring and circle once or twice to establish your pace, balance, and rhythm.

After you've organized yourself and your horse, plan your approach to the first fence with as many straight strides as possible, so you have plenty of room for smooth adjustments. Before you turn toward the line, focus on the center of the first fence as this rider is doing here (your peripheral vision will keep

you aware of the track your horse is actually on).

While you're on the short side of your arena, hold your horse on your outside rein, using your inside leg and a little indirect inside rein if he tends to cut in with his inside shoulder. You should feel him traveling evenly between your hands and legs, in a chute created by your aids. You'll want to keep this even feel throughout any course of jumps, whether you're on a straight track or turning.

2. Begin your turn when you see the route that will bring you in line with the center of the first fence. (Avoid hugging the rail so long that you overshoot the line.) Use both reins—inside opening rein and outside steady rein—to make your turn, and to maintain an even feel of both sides of your horse's mouth.

Keep your inside leg at the girth to hold him on the curving track. As you come through the final segment of the turn, move your outside leg slightly behind the girth and apply pressure to maintain impulsion and hold his hindquarters on the track.

If your horse tends to weave or drift, keep him straight with your reins—but don't take back with them, since he can't travel straight if he isn't going forward. Instead, maintain his forward rhythm while you apply an opening rein as needed; then return to the chute created by your even hand and leg pressure.

3. You may find that, like many riders lacking confidence over fences, you instinctively close your fingers on the reins to shorten your horse's stride when you turn to a fence, as this rider is doing here. If you fall into this habit of taking back, you'll soon see nothing but incredibly short distances and find yourself riding off your hands to every fence instead of using your horse's active, forward rhythm.

To keep yourself from taking back, practice loosening up as you come out of the short end. Consciously release all the tension in your arms and hands; let your horse's canter rhythm take you to the jump. As he realizes you're not going to get in his way, he'll stay softer as he approaches the jump and make his own adjustments smoothly.

DETERMINING STRIDE LENGTH

Before you begin work on the six-stride line that forms the basis of this lesson, you need to know the length of your horse's stride; not its measurement in feet, but whether it's normal, short, or long. If you've ridden a variety of horses, you can probably tell whether his stride is short and rapid, long and sweeping, or average. If you're not sure, check stride length in the following way:

➤ Set two jump rails on the ground, 60 feet apart (which is five normal canter strides without jumps, measured as 20 of your three-foot course-walking strides).

➤ Pick up your normal working canter, ride in over the first pole, and count the number of strides your horse takes before going out over the second with no adjustment from you.

➤ If he does it in six, you know he has a short stride.

➤ If his toes almost touch the second pole on stride five, he has a long stride.

➤ If he canters comfortably out over the second pole, he has a normal stride.

How your horse meets the first pole—very close or standing way back—could influence your count, so canter the exercise two or three times to check your initial impression.

4. As you near the jump, try to see your distance. Remember, though, that adjusting stride means assuming a new responsibility: Any change you make must complement your horse's efforts, not take away from them.

Therefore, if you can tell your stride isn't quite right but you're not sure how to adjust it, stay still and keep watching the jump. You'll be able to tell whether you're short or long as you come nearer; meanwhile, your horse will have enough balance to make his own adjustment. The next time you see the same "off" distance, you'll probably recognize the adjustment you need to make.

5. If you're certain you can help your horse by shortening or lengthening his stride, aim to do the least amount necessary at the earliest possible moment to gain the results you want. That way, the closer you come to the jump, the less you're doing. Consider both the kind of immediate adjustment you need to make and the effect that adjustment will have on the line following the jump.

To keep your adjustments invisible and to make your horse as easy to ride as possible, resist the urge to run at that long distance. Instead, close your fingers and add a stride (shown here), as you did in your earliest exercises with the pole on the ground, maintaining sufficient leg to preserve his rhythmic canter. Keep him soft and balanced now—again, you're forming a habit—so you'll be more likely to keep him that way to the end of his last line on a real course.

If the distance appears just a little longer than your horse's stride, lighten your firm feel on the reins—but don't open your fingers. Depending on your horse's temperament, add leg to back up the message from your hands. Apply the aids smoothly so he extends his stride's length rather than increasing its speed.

Concentrate on the jump and return to your normal hand and leg pressure the instant you sense you've adjusted enough (most adjustments can be made quietly over two or three strides). If you overdo, you'll end up too close to the fence.

6. In the air over the fence, your responsibilities are the same whether your spot was good or bad: to stay off your horse's back and off his mouth, and to focus your eyes and your thinking on the second fence. A poor takeoff causes problems in the line, but you can begin correcting for it while you're in the air. If your horse left the ground from a short distance and lost impulsion, cluck as he pushes off or while he's in the air, to encourage him to jump out across the fence with more effort. If his takeoff was long, use a "whoa" in the air to steady him in the landing stride and remove some of his extra pace.

7. If you met the first jump comfortably out of stride, landed into your legs, and used your hand and leg to reorganize your horse in the control stride, you have very little work to do inside the line. Stay in your balanced two-point position, main-

tain an active canter as our horse and rider are doing here, and you'll meet the second jump perfectly.

8. However, if you found a short distance coming in, your horse probably slowed down as he shortened, reducing the length of his arc over the first fence and

landing closer to it than if he'd jumped from a normal distance. To make the six work smoothly, apply leg in the control stride as our rider is doing here—how much, and with what combination of hand aids, you'll learn by experimenting.

Most horses move up enough in the first three strides; if yours does, you'll be able to coast smoothly through the last three strides to a perfect takeoff spot. With a quick horse, you may find that you only need to move up on the control stride; if your horse is very quiet, you may need to move up over four. Next time, remember the degree of leg aid you used and increase or decrease, so you get the adjustment you want in three strides.

If you do too much—you routinely move him up over all six strides and leg him off the ground—you'll make him dependent on you, so he stops trying on his own. So continue experimenting with the lightest aids that work; they'll probably be similar to those you apply on the flat. By adjusting early and smoothly, you'll avoid that white-knuckle question: "Am I going to get the six?" and make it look effortless.

experiment to see what degree of rein and upper-body aids are needed to get the stride shortening you need to smoothly ride the line.

10. Before your horse takes off over the second fence, focus your eyes and attention on the end of the ring and on your strategy for the upcoming straight-away and turn. Even though you aren't going to meet another line now, establish the good habits you'll

9. If your horse's stride is naturally long, or he jumped in with exuber-ance, you'll need to "tap the brakes" early to avoid a hasty slow-down in front of the second fence. In the control stride, and through the first three strides if necessary, sit up and feel his mouth, until you feel his stride short-en slightly. Then relax your aids and maintain the stride to the second fence. As with lengthen-ing stride, you'll have to

need when you do. After you land, aim to get all your reorganizing done before you reach the turn, so that by halfway around the short end you're as organized as you were when you turned to approach your first fence.

11. Left to himself, your horse may land on the wrong lead, as this horse has, and/or begin turning almost immediately. Even if he stays on a straight track for a few more strides, he may fall in through his inside shoulder when he does turn. By the midpoint of the short end, he might be unbalanced and inattentive, looking down to the ground or out beyond the rail of your ring instead of ahead to his next fence.

Again, use your control stride; no matter which lead your horse landed on, hold him on a straight track so he can't cut in, and balance him in preparation for the upcoming corner. Try to feel whether he's on the correct lead, so you don't disturb his balance or influence him to leave the straight track (with a little practice, you'll soon be able to tell which shoulder is leading). If you can't, use your peripheral vision.

12. If, as is likely, you need to change leads, do it deliberately and before you reach the corner. First sit up smoothly and bring your horse together, so he's straight and balanced on the outside lead, and you have control of his pace and track. If he tends to fall to the inside, use an inside indirect rein and an opening outside rein to hold him straight.

A couple of strides (or sooner) from the end wall, ask for the change. Keep an equal feel in both reins, moving them slightly to the inside. Maintain pressure in your inside leg to prevent your horse from cutting in as you signal for the change. Then release that pressure as you move your outside leg back and ask for the lead change.

Avoid pulling or jerking up on your inside rein at the same time. This not only creates an unattractive picture but also unbalances the horse, so he may change only in front. If your horse is green or difficult to change, you can apply slightly stronger aids; also, see Lesson 6: Fix That Funky Flying Lead Change, page 61.

If you get the change but your horse quickens, softly stop him, to erase his "forward" thought. (Avoid doing so abruptly, or he may think he's being punished for the change.) Next time, modify your aid a little, depending on what you've learned about his reactions. Then use the turn to subtly slow him and compensate for any loss of balance from the change.

If you need to use a touch of spur a few times to get the change, don't grab back when your horse speeds up. Let him go forward on a circle; use your voice and close your fingers to regroup softly. If, without losing balance, you repeatedly slow him down before the change—and you don't punish him for speeding up after it—he'll gradually become less anxious about the movement.

13. Even if your horse is a little strong, soften your hands and make him look softer than he feels (as you will when you show). Encourage him to soften by easing your contact for a brief moment in each stride, as you sit up to help him balance rearward. As you do, run through your mental checklists and make any final adjustments of position, rhythm, and balance. By the midpoint of your long side, look through the turn to where a new line would be, then bring your horse to a walk and give him a pat.

Continue practicing the six-stride line until you're meeting both fences from a comfortable distance, accurately assessing the adjustment you'll

need to make to the second fence from the distance you see to the first. You can keep the work interesting for your horse by placing the line in a different area of your ring, varying the types of jumps you use, or raising height. (If you use two verticals, you can jump the line from either direction.) You'll find that no matter how different the jumps look, the principles you've learned still apply.

If you run into any trouble, say your horse starts rushing his fences, stopping at them, or drifting in the line, turn to Lesson 15: Troubleshooting Tips, page 131.

Adjustability

LEARN TO ADJUST YOUR HORSE'S STRIDE IN ORDER TO MEET
LONG OR SHORT DISTANCES, IN THIS CONFIDENCE-BUILDING
WARM-UP TO OUR FUTURE COURSE-WORK LESSON.

Bonus: Our Clip-and-Save Distance Chart!

In our last lesson, you practiced riding a line based on a normal, 12-foot stride, or one that matched your own horse's natural step. Now we're going to graduate up a level, and have you work on lines that are longer and shorter than normal.

That's because in hunter, equitation, and jumping classes, course designers may test your horse's adjustability by setting some lines normal, some short, and some long. That means you need to learn to adjust your horse's stride to fit varying lines. (For more information, see "The Long And Short of Distances," page 102.)

The work you've done on the flat and in previous lessons, in which you fit different numbers of strides between poles on the ground, will pay dividends now. As you did in the pole exercises, you'll preserve your horse's rhythm, balance, and track when you ask for lengthening or shortening. But you'll need to change two elements: his pace and your eye.

Think of pace as impulsion: the degree of contained energy in your horse's stride, not its speed. If you have trouble creating more energy without going faster, think in terms of relaxed power. You'll lengthen stride by increasing your horse's energy level with leg pressure, then softening your feel on his mouth to let his stride cover more ground.

To shorten, you'll reduce impulsion by closing your fingers and lightening your leg pressure. As you compress and expand the spring that your hands and legs create, you should notice a change in the amount of ground each stride covers, rather than a drastic change in speed.

Your eye, the second variable you need to change, has become used to seeing distances to low fences out of a normal stride, thanks to our previous lessons. You've learned to "feel" whether your approach is right or wrong as you near each fence by sensing whether your normal stride will divide evenly into the space between you and your takeoff spot.

Now your eye will have to adapt to dividing the space into longer and shorter lengths as well. At first you'll probably feel more comfortable with lines that are set short: The increments are easier to visualize, and the shortened stride gives you more time to adjust. It may take longer to develop an eye for long distances, but gradually you'll come to see that the incremental distance gives you a stride not much greater than the stride you use in the normal lines you're riding comfortably.

With short and long distances, however, the consequences of mistakes can be more serious, so

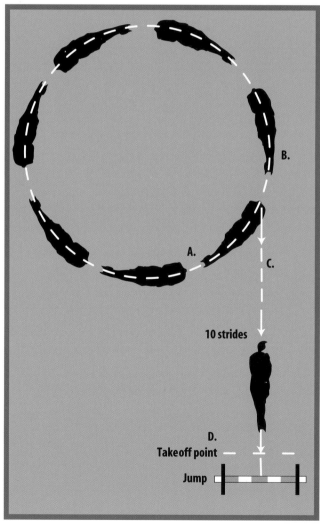

Exercise 1: Shortened Stride to a Single

your skills will have to be sharp. So, before you begin this lesson, see "Skill Check," at right. Until you can satisfy all those requirements, don't start the new work. Instead, continue with your previous lessons until you can.

WHAT YOU'LL NEED:
- ➤ A flat, level work area with good footing, with room to set up to a six-stride line.
- ➤ Enough standards and rails to set up to two fences for a line.

EXERCISE 1:
SHORTENED STRIDE TO A SINGLE

Before you try to hold a short stride through a line of two jumps, use this exercise to practice maintaining a short stride on the flat, and over a single jump. It will help you get used to the pace of a short line. Bonus: It'll teach you to look for a more comfortable distance when the first one you see is long and awkward.

A. Place a single 2-foot fence so you can meet it from a 10-stride approach off a circle at the end of your ring. (See diagram at left.) Establish your normal canter on the circle, then take just enough of a feel of your horse's mouth to shorten his stride a few inches without losing rhythm or balance.

Continue circling, running through your pace-rhythm-track checklist as you start each new lap. When you complete your circle, you should feel as if you could go straight to the jump. Your canter should feel active and accurate, with no loss in impulsion.

B. When you've maintained your slightly shortened stride for two or three laps, turn your eyes to the jump and leave the circle. Your preparation is done; all you have to do is maintain the rhythm and balance.

Look for your takeoff spot out of the pace you have. It should be just about the same spot you've been using all along. If you realize you aren't quite

SKILL CHECK

Avoid beginning this lesson until you can check all the following boxes as affirmative:

❏ You can maintain the correct pace, balance, rhythm, and track—not just on a circle, but down a line with a normal distance and on around the end of the ring. If you need more than one control stride to regroup after the first fence on a line, you'll have trouble maintaining the quality of your horse's stride and meeting the remaining fences safely.

❏ Your base of support is solid from heels through hips, giving you dependable control of your upper body as well as your lower body. Up to this point you've stayed safe enough by maintaining your two-point position and sinking your weight into your heels. Now, however, you're also going to need upper-body security so you don't find yourself losing your position when your horse lengthens stride.

❏ You can tell when you're six strides from any fence on a normal line, and can ride a straight track to the center of every jump. To ride this lesson's long lines, you're going to need to see both distances and approaches more quickly than ever before, so your eye must be at least 90 percent reliable in seeing normal distances.

❏ You can use a soft release and maintain a light feel of your horse's mouth over the jump without interfering with his balance, so you can smoothly regain control in the landing (control) stride. If you're still pushing your hands forward and letting him jump with loopy reins, you won't be able to influence the lead he lands on or use the control stride fully.

❏ You can adjust your horse's trot and canter easily and have a good idea of how much pressure you need to apply or lighten for a small adjustment and for a larger one.

❏ When you lighten your feel on your horse's mouth and increase leg pressure, he instantly begins covering more ground. When you decrease leg pressure and close your fingers, he shortens his stride without losing energy.

THE LONG AND SHORT OF DISTANCES

Use these insights to better understand why adjustability is critical to riding a successful course.

➤ **Normal = 12 feet.** Normal distances, like the ones you rode in the last lesson, are composed of 12-foot increments (the length of the average horse's canter stride), plus an allowance for takeoff and landing. However, some lines don't conform to normal length of stride. For any of several reasons, they ride long or short.

➤ **When adjusting, think inches.** The difference per stride will be a matter of inches, not feet. For instance, in a six-stride line, your horse may only need to extend or compress each of his strides by 4 or 6 inches. Even if the adjustment per stride is as much as 12 inches, you won't have to gallop or mince to ride the line comfortably.

➤ **Know your lines.** Other factors besides the physical spacing of fences may influence a line to ride long or short. In fact, the same line may ride differently depending on where it is and where in the course you meet it. For instance, a line that walks normally and rides normally as the first line (heading away from the gate) may ride a little snug as the last line, when your horse is (eagerly) heading for home. In fact, any final line is likely to ride a little shorter than it walked for this reason.

➤ **Indoors, or out?** A line in a small ring or an indoor arena rides longer than one set with the same distance in a large open field because your horse instinctively adapts his stride to his surroundings. His normal stride in the open may be several inches longer than his normal stride in a small ring. (It's useful, therefore, to try him in several settings and find out what effect different environments have on his striding.)

right but aren't sure whether to lengthen or shorten, do neither. Maintain the stride, rhythm, and balance, keep up your impulsion, and your horse will make the spot work out safely.

C. If you see what's needed, help your horse shorten a little or lengthen a few inches for a couple of strides. If you see a very long spot soon after you turn onto the straight approach, resist the temptation to run down to it. Sit quietly for another stride and wait for a quieter distance.

Even if you don't like what you see, avoid pulling up or circling out from the jump. Doing so can easily become a crutch that you lean on every time you don't like a distance. It won't teach you or your horse to cope with awkward distances, and it may make your horse a stopper.

You can circle if your horse loses his pace just as he begins the straight approach. If it happens closer to the jump, just sit still, hold him together, and cluck to tell him to go forward.

D. If you have trouble visualizing your takeoff spot from the shorter stride, gouge a line in the dirt with your heel 2 feet in front of the jump. Focus on the jump, not the ground, as you approach; your peripheral vision will keep you aware of the line.

When you feel confident about maintaining a short stride, test yourself by circling just once before you approach the jump. If you can keep the short stride on the circle and throughout your approach, with no further adjustment beyond a little fine-tuning to get the takeoff spot you want, you're ready to advance to the next exercise.

EXERCISE 2: SHORTENED STRIDE IN A LINE

Now you're going to work on maintaining the short stride down a line of two jumps. Eighty-two feet from the single fence, add another vertical or an oxer of the same height. You now have a line with six short strides. Gouge a line in the dirt 2 feet in front of each jump to mark your takeoff target. (See diagram, opposite page.)

A line set this way is 2 feet shorter than a normal one. If

your horse has a 12-foot canter, you'll need to shorten an average of 4 inches per stride. (If his stride is shorter than normal, you won't need to shorten quite so much; if it's longer, you'll need to remove a few additional inches.)

As you did in the first exercise, begin by cantering a circle. Go from a normal canter stride to a shorter one without changing your balance, rhythm, or track. As long as you focus on maintaining these qualities, the distance will work out. Even if the stride doesn't stay uniformly short, your horse will be able to jump out of the line comfortably.

CLIP-AND-SAVE DISTANCE CHART

So how do you determine if a line is set long or short? You use a course-walking stride. That is, you step off the distance using a 3-foot walk stride (if your horse has a normal 12-foot canter stride; a little more or less if he's short- or long-strided). That way, you can set distances, or establish the distance of the lines you'll be riding.

This chart is a guide to setting and walking off distances, and is per United States Equestrian Federation guidelines. Distance is measured from the top rail of a vertical and from the middle of the spread of an oxer.

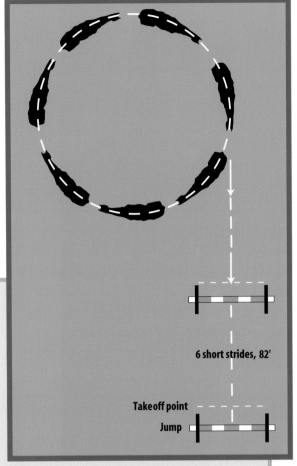

6 short strides, 82'

Takeoff point

Jump

Exercise 2: Shortened Stride in a Line

FENCE HEIGHT AND STRIDE LENGTH	3' FENCE 12' STRIDE	3'6" FENCE 12'3" STRIDE	3'6" FENCE 12'6" STRIDE	3'6" FENCE 12'9" STRIDE
# OF STRIDES				
1	25'6"	26'	26'	26'
2	36'6"	37'	37'	37'
3	48'	48'9"	49'6"	50'3"
4	60'	61'	62'	63'
5	72'	73'3"	74'6"	75'9"
6	84'	85'6"	87'	88'6"
7	96'	97'9"	99'6"	101'3"

1. As you approach the first fence, aim for a normal takeoff spot. If you see a long one, canter another stride with the same pace to find a more relaxed distance. If you see a short distance, support your horse to it by maintaining your leg and rein aids and staying over his center of gravity.

2. As you support him for the short one, keep a soft, consistent leg contact, encouraging him to reach under his body with his hindquarters, and use a soft but definite feel to prevent him from increasing speed or stride length as he nears the fence.

   Some quiet horses lose impulsion coming into a short distance off a short stride. If yours arrives at the takeoff spot a little dead, use a cluck and a touch more leg pressure to encourage him to jump across

KEEP YOUR SHOULDERS BACK!

You probably hear that a lot. Why is it so key? Your horse is like a rear-engine car: His power base is behind you. If you put him to a short distance and lean forward, running your hands up his neck, you'll throw his balance onto his forehand. He'll have to jump straight up; unless he's very athletic, he won't use his shoulders. He'll leave his knees down (as the horse below is doing) and land in a heap, with no impulsion.

If you lean forward like this while asking him to jump from a long distance, chances are he'll "chip," meaning he'll add an awkward short stride before the fence (as shown at left)—or even stop. That's because as soon as your horse feels your body weight come forward, no matter how light you are, he'll feel unbalanced and shift his weight onto his forehand, making it difficult for him to rock back over his hind end and jump.

You can see why keeping your shoulders back, and waiting for the fence to come to you out of a balanced, rhythmic stride, is always your best bet!

Error! Shoulders too far forward.

the fence. When you're more secure, you may want to lay your stick behind your leg in the air to help him land with impulsion.

As you take off, assess the effect your spot will have on the line. If you took off from a good distance, you'll probably land where you expected to, so you won't need to do anything but preserve the pace you began with. If your horse jumped bigger than you expected, you'll need to steady him more in the control stride. If he jumped below the pace, you'll need to restore his energy once he lands, just as you did in our last lesson.

3. Land solidly into your legs, so your base of support absorbs the shock of the jump. As your horse's front feet touch down, open up your hip angle a little to be sure you don't land on his neck.

4. As his hind legs land and his forelegs reach forward into the control stride, softly regain contact with his mouth without snatching his head. Don't just land and start counting strides. Use the control stride to check whether your horse's rhythm and balance feel right. If they don't, you won't be able to depend on his giving you the adjustments you may need. If he lands a little dead and close to the fence, regain your pace by closing your leg and softening your hand to let him lengthen his stride, then softly close your fingers to contain his energy.

5. If he feels a little strong when you land, regain your pace by closing your hand and lightening your legs to compress his stride, as our rider is doing here. When you've

6

Too much drilling of short distances might make your horse lose his willingness to move forward, so set a six-stride line with a normal distance elsewhere in your ring. Alternate between the short and normal lines until you're comfortable riding both of them. Then experiment with different degrees of "short"—everything from 3 to 12 inches a stride. You can use lines of three, four, or five strides as well as six; just work on establishing a stride that lets you hit your normal takeoff comfortably.

TIP

reestablished rhythm and balance in the same shortened stride you used approaching the first fence, your homework is done. Hold your horse's canter together while you count strides and watch the new distance.

6. The first several times through this exercise, you may not see your second takeoff spot until you're rather close to it. You'll be preoccupied with other things during your landing and control strides, and your eye will be trying to adapt to the shorter stride.

After riding the line several times, you'll begin feeling how much shortening you need to make the distance work smoothly. With practice your eye will adapt to the new stride length; you'll feel the relationship of stride to distance earlier and earlier. Eventually you'll see in your control stride exactly what you must do to make the line work.

You don't have to be perfect to advance to the next exercise. As soon as you feel safe, you're ready to move on.

EXERCISE 3:
LENGTHEN IN A LINE

Now that you can comfortably handle short distances in a line, you're going to work with long distances. To minimize any urge you might feel to run at your fences, you'll lengthen stride in small, easy increments, beginning with inches per stride. The measurements given in this exercise are for a horse with a 12-foot canter stride.

If yours is shorter strided, adjust the distance between fences so you're only asking him to extend his normal stride by 4 inches. And any time you're lengthening, consider the combined effect of your horse's natural stride and his reaction time. If he's slow to react to your lengthening aids and short-strided, you'll have to adjust more to compensate for a long distance than you will if he has an average stride and responds quickly.

Move the second fence from Exercise 2 out 4 feet, so the line measures 86 feet from top rail to top rail. (See diagram at right.) This will give you room for six 12-foot-4-inch strides between the landing and takeoff.

Use the circle from Exercise 1 to establish the correct pace as you apply enough leg pressure to lengthen your horse's stride by 4 inches. You should feel him pick up his speed a few miles per hour from his normal active canter, but not so much that he's galloping.

He doesn't need a vast amount more energy to lengthen stride by 4 inches, but he does need some to maintain his rhythm and balance. When you feel his quarters reaching more energetically under his body and his stride covering a little more ground, you're ready to turn to the jump.

7. As you canter toward the fence, try to visualize whether your longer stride will divide evenly into the distance. The picked-up pace will help you think and see in longer terms, and the distance you eat up with every stride will help you interpret what you're seeing. If you feel sure an adjustment will give you a smoother takeoff spot, close your fingers more firmly or lighten your feel—but don't lean forward in an attempt to "help" him lengthen. (For why, see "Keep Your Shoulders Back!", at page 104.)

8. Since your horse's stride is now longer and his pace greater, you may see a takeoff spot that's a bit farther out, as our rider is here. You don't have to make any more effort with your body to stay with your horse from a spot that's a little long. Just keep your balanced two-point position . . .

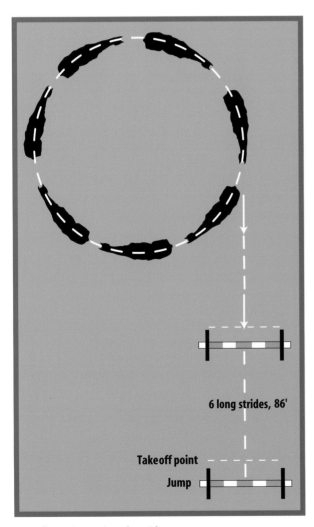

6 long strides, 86'

Takeoff point

Jump

Exercise 3: Lengthen in a Line

9. …and let him close the angles between his body and yours. If your horse jumps in stride, give or take a few inches, he'll probably land with his pace intact. Check on the pace in the control stride; then you can sit quietly and watch the second fence, counting strides as you near it.

However, if your landing is a little quiet—your horse jumped from too long a spot or lost impulsion,

you'll need to make up for it. You can do this in one of two ways:

➤ If your horse has a normal stride and lengthens easily, you can ask him to lengthen slightly through all six strides and be confident of reaching the second fence at a comfortable takeoff spot.

➤ If you're not sure how easily he'll make the longer distance, reassure yourself by moving up a generous amount in each of the first three strides. Then you can sit quietly for the last three, waiting for the spot to happen.

As your ability to maintain his pace and track improves, place a normal line on one side of your ring and a short or long one on the other. Use a circle to prepare for the normal line; leave the circle when you're satisfied with your pace and balance. When you finish the line, repeat your organizing routine. If you don't need to circle again, continue directly to the next line—but be sure to use the end of your ring to adjust, without changing rhythm, to an appropriate pace for the new distance.

Moving up in the early strides may pay off if your horse is the rangy, long-necked type. Such animals find it harder to balance when they lengthen stride than do short, compact ones. Moving a rangy horse up over the first three strides gives you the last three to balance him for his jump; knowing he's in balance, you'll be more confident about his ability.

Bending Lines

LEARN TO MASTER A BENDING LINE, USING THESE
CONFIDENCE-BOOSTING STRATEGIES.

Finding a distance is easier on a straight track than on a bending one. That's why, so far, you've met the centers of all your fences straight on. That's about to change. Why?

When the route between two fences is a bending line (meaning the fences are slightly offset)—something you'll likely encounter in the hunter, equitation, and jumper rings—you may have the option of meeting each fence on a slight angle. At the very least, your track won't be the straight line we've been practicing.

You may find the thought of riding such a line frightening; many riders do. Relax! With the skills you've learned, and the confidence you've built thus far, you're set up to succeed. And I'll help you every step of the way.

To that end, before we begin this lesson, perform the warm-up outlined in Lesson 13, on page 115. And, review "5 Factors For In-Line Success," at right. Then we'll tackle the art of riding a bending line.

WHAT YOU'LL NEED:

➤ A level work area with good footing, large enough to set up a six-stride bending line.

➤ Enough standards and poles for two fences.

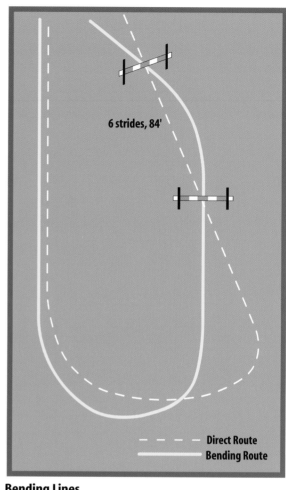

6 strides, 84'

--- Direct Route
——— Bending Route

Bending Lines

Riding Bending Lines

A. THE BENDING ROUTE (ADDING A STRIDE)

1. To work on bending lines, set two low fences six strides apart from center to center, on a direct route, as shown in the diagram above. When you opt to add a stride, make a straight approach to the first fence, as shown.

5 FACTORS FOR IN-LINE SUCCESS

How you ride the turn leading to a regular or bending line is critical to your success in the line.
Five factors will determine the track you'll select:

I. The distance you see to the first fence. It's easier to find a long spot by riding to the inside track of the turn to your first jump. (See diagram below.) It's easier to find a short one by moving slightly to the outside of the track. With either option, you can still meet your first fence straight on.

Riding an inside track is similar to riding a direct route on a bending line. It gets you to the jump more quickly than the long, bending curve you'd make to take a wider approach, essentially "leaving out" a stride. So, if you see a longish distance to the first fence that's comfortable for the pace you have, begin your turn to the fence a couple of feet early.

II. The distance in the line. Approach the first fence in a pace and stride appropriate for the way the line is set—is it normal, meaning based on a 12-foot canter stride? Or, is it set short, or long? (For more information on adjustability in lines, see Lesson 11: Adjustability, page 99.)

For instance, if you see a long distance but you know the line calls for a steady, quiet stride, don't turn early. Instead, canter another stride before you turn and look for a quieter distance that's better suited to the pace you want between the fences. Take the inside track only if you see the distance early or the line is long (see number III, below, for an exception to this factor).

III. The location of the line. Here's the exception to the inside-track advice I just gave you (above): If the inside track would require you to turn at an acute angle—say the line is set on the diagonal, for example—taking it would defeat your purpose. The tight turn could compress your horse's stride and make you miss the longer spot. Guiding him quietly around the outside track will give you a smoother performance.

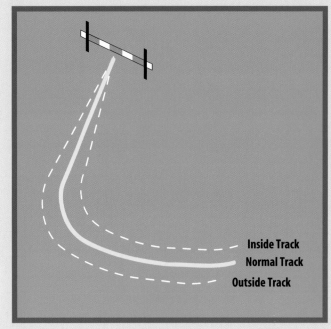

Inside Track
Normal Track
Outside Track

IV. Your horse's level of education. If your horse is green, turning takes longer; you probably won't be able to use the inside track to a long spot. Also, avoid choosing the inside track with a horse that tends to drift or tries to move sideways; it could encourage him to cut in.

The more schooled your horse becomes, the faster he'll respond, until he's practically turning in answer to your head movement. And the more responsive he is, the more you'll be able to choose a track to suit what you see.

V. The route between the two fences. When the route between two fences is a bending line, you may make an exception to the 90-degree approach rule. Most bending lines give you an option: You can leave out a stride and ride the direct route from center to center, meeting both fences at a slight angle—which gives you a long distance. Or, you can meet the first fence straight, drift out a stride in the line, and meet the second straight at a normal distance. The added-stride option is the wiser choice if your horse's stride is somewhat limited.

2. A stride before take-off, or at the latest, over the jump, turn your head to look at the center of the second fence; your eye control will guide you onto the correct track.

3. When you land, use your inside-leg-to-outside-rein aids, to press your horse onto the outside of the track while you watch the second jump and count seven strides. (You added one with your bending line.)

4. As soon as you see you've opened up room for the additional stride, relax your leg pressure and guide him to the center of the fence.

B. THE DIRECT ROUTE (SIX STRIDES)

5. If you choose the direct route, plan a track that lets you jump the first fence…

6. …at a slightly oblique angle (still jumping at the center of the fence).

7. Then take the shortest route (a straight, diagonal line; see diagram)…

8. … to the center of the second jump. To make the finish after your line look neat, continue on the same diagonal track for a few strides, before guiding your horse on the track to your next fence.

When you're confident riding bending lines, mix an occasional bending line in with normal, short, and average lines of varying lengths that you're stringing together. Try riding several different lines in succession, as you will on a course.

If necessary, give yourself a chance to regroup by riding a circle and running through your pace-rhythm-track checklist. Make it a habit to soften your feel of your horse's mouth for two or three strides on the short side, even if he's a little tense—remember, the more you pull, the more he'll pull. (For more information on dealing with strong horses and other problems, see Lesson 15: Troubleshooting Tips, page 131.)

You may find the thought of riding such a line frightening; many riders do. Relax! With the skills you've learned, and the confidence you've built thus far, you're set up to succeed. And I'll help you every step of the way.

Course-Work Warm-Up

MAKE SURE YOUR HORSE—AND YOU—ARE READY, WILLING, AND ABLE TO TACKLE A COURSE, WITH THIS BE-PREPARED WARM-UP ON THE FLAT AND OVER FENCES.

A warm-up's purpose is threefold:

I. It enables your horse to limber up his joints and muscles so he can perform at his athletic best.

II. It provides you with a "pre-flight check" covering his responses to your aids, on the flat and over fences.

III. It allows you to check your own flatwork and jumping position.

Problems found here can be nipped in the bud before you start jumping a course. Plus, this warm-up tests your own mental readiness for jumping. When your horse is limbered up and responsive, chances are you'll have the confidence to jump. And that's the point of all these lessons!

The following set of exercises, each a bit more demanding than the last, can help you accomplish those aims. Before you begin, please check out the points in "Warm-Up Wisdom," page 121.

WHAT YOU'LL NEED:

➤ A level work area with good footing.

➤ Enough standards and poles to make two warm-up fences.

Flat Work

Walk your horse for 5 to 10 minutes (more if he's stiff) on light contact, to increase his circulation without adding stress. Ask for an active, purposeful, marching walk, each leg reaching forward and pushing against the ground, so he really loosens his joints and muscles.

Start on a straight track or a generous (at least 60-foot) circle. After a few minutes, ask for several turns to check his responses to your aids. An S-turn through a circle, a half-circle reverse, and a turn across a diagonal will tell you whether your horse is listening to your legs and hands. (If he's not, apply them slightly firmer until he is.)

Check his reactions further by asking him to halt, then walk forward again. When he responds to your aids for these simple movements and maintains his active walk without undue prompting, pick up the trot. (If he's sluggish, sharpen his response with a touch of your spur or crop.)

1. Staying off the rail, if you have one (so you know your horse is responding to you, not it), warm up in the trot for about 5 minutes. Ask him to start out at the trot with his neck stretching slightly down, into your contact (as shown above), and his hind end tracking up under him, with energy. This will stretch and supple his neck, back, and hindquarters.

Guide him on a straight track or a large circle, in both directions, to encourage him thinking "forward." (If he's naturally forward, guide him onto a smaller circle.)

2. When your horse feels supple (soft in your hand, and moving forward off your leg), slightly increase your rein and leg contact to compress him into the light degree of collection shown here—the degree you'd need for a turn on course. Then test his responsiveness in more demanding figures. These can include smaller circles, spiral circles (great for getting him to move away from inside and outside leg aids), half-circles, S-turns, and serpentines.

Check your horse's adjustability by asking him to lengthen and shorten his stride several times in the trot. When he shortens in response to increased finger pressure and lengthens as soon as you lighten your feel and add a leg squeeze, add some downward transitions.

Ask your horse to walk, by sitting up and increasing your finger pressure on the reins. Walk five or six strides, then squeeze with your legs to step him into the trot. Not only does this reinforce adjustability and responsiveness, it also gets your horse working even more from his hindquarters, which will help when we begin jumping.

3. Now check your horse's responsiveness at the canter. Begin at your normal working canter stride, alternating between circles and straight tracks on both leads, to be sure he moves forward from your leg and bends through the turns.

Then shorten and lengthen his stride, as you did at the trot (and will have to on course). When your horse maintains his balance consistently through these adjustments, ask for a lead change in each direction.

Before you move on to the jumping phase of your warm-up, test your preparedness: Cantering on a circle, pretend you're about to leave it to jump a fence, as shown in the above photo. If you can visualize yourself riding a comfortable track to the obstacle, you're ready for the next exercise.

FLATWORK—WHY BOTHER?

If I had a horse that moved incredibly well, was naturally balanced, was well off his forehand, carried himself *and* had a beautiful round outline, I'd likely have a minimalist flatwork program.

After all, since jumping is really just flatwork with fences in the way, that horse wouldn't need much help from me to jump a course beautifully.

However, I don't own such a horse. Nor do I have clients who can easily spend $500,000 on a fabulous German-trained horse that comes "ready made" this way.

So if you're like my clients and me, we have to get that balance and self-carriage ourselves. Why bother?

➤ He'll be "connected" from his front end through his hind end— that is, his body will be rounded like a Slinky toy, with his weight shifted over his hindquarters, his back lifted under your seat, and his shoulders elevated. He won't be hollowed out along his back, with his weight on his forehand. (See Photo A, above.)

➤ A horse who carries himself like this finds any event easier (be it jumpers, hunters, or eventing), because he's *balanced*.

➤ He'll develop proper muscling, resulting in better movement (more "step" and prettier gaits).

➤ By tracking under himself with his hind legs, he'll lighten his front end. This enables him to shorten and lengthen his stride more easily than a strung-out horse, and to push off the ground more easily when jumping. (That means a prettier jump.)

➤ He'll be more comfortable to ride than a strung-out horse, because his gaits will be rhythmic and elastic, rather than stilted and choppy.

➤ He'll travel with his body straight—which is critical for jumping courses—because he is moving forward from his hindquarters.

Okay, so now you're saying, "I'm convinced…but how do I achieve all this?" Softly close your leg while taking an equally soft contact with your reins. Ask him to walk forward with rhythmical steps, staying soft in your hands.

If he leans on you, avoid punishing his mouth (that would be the wrong end). Instead, add more leg and tell him to step under himself, creating impulsion. This causes him to carry his own front end, and his mouth will lighten. You'll feel less pressure on the reins as his weight shifts to his back legs.

At the trot, squeeze your legs in the rhythm in which you want the horse to trot (kind of a boom, boom, boom trot), then gradually use less leg and see if he'll maintain it without a reminder, even for a few steps.

As you apply leg, maintain your rein contact. You don't want him to simply trot faster and become strung out. You want him "connected," which ultimately produces true flexion. (You'll see this connectedness in Photo B, above.)

The technique for the canter is the same. Sit centered above him and combine downward transitions with an occasional halt and back, which makes your horse step under himself, thus lightening his front end.

Then immediately squeeze him back into a canter, to capture his energy and propel it forward. It is as if you're opening the front door and pushing him through it. When you feel the energy carrying you (he's light in your hand, and moving forward from his hind end with minimal leg aids from you), he's connected.

On a personal note, I will not ride a horse that I can't easily balance over jumps. I think it's extremely difficult to find a distance on a horse that's strung out, on his forehand, and leaning on my hands. Call it "Old School." I call it "broke."

Add a Crossrail

Jumping a crossrail before you tackle a course will help you catch and correct any problem with your position or your horse's responsiveness before you get into trouble.

4. Pick up an energetic working trot on a circle, then exit the circle on a straight track to the crossrail. Post down to the jump, to help your horse maintain his rhythm and balance; maintain light contact, and allow him to find his own takeoff point.

Each time you land, follow the track out straight; then circle and come back the other way. If your horse trots softly down to the fence and lands cantering, let him continue for several strides; then bring him back to a trot before circling back to the jump.

5. If he's strong in the approach, trying to drag you to the jump, stop him soon after he lands. Avoid doing so with anger; just be firm (as this rider is demonstrating). *Now* is the time to let him know a strong approach is unacceptable. If you were to let it go at a single crossrail, he'd soon be barrelling around a course in our next lesson.

6. If he lands a little dead from the crossrail, and trots away from it rather than cantering, firmly send him forward into a quiet, active canter. Avoid overreacting. Sending him into a wild gallop will just upset him.

If he doesn't move forward willingly from your leg, add a cluck and a nudge of your spur or reach back and tap him with your stick behind your leg, as shown.

The attitude you establish over the crossrail in your warm-up will carry over to all the jumping that follows, so don't advance until he's listening to your aids in the approach.

Trot the crossrail four to six times, or until your horse is approaching it with a relaxed, responsive attitude. Only then should you graduate to the next warm-up phase: Jumping a vertical.

Warm Up Over a Vertical

7. Change the crossrail to a 2-foot vertical. Trot this fence two or three times. Each time you go over the vertical, mentally check your position and your horse's responsiveness. If he speeds up or slows down over this fence, see the earlier corrections.

Now that you've jumped six to nine fences out of a trot—enough to warm up your horse's jumping mechanism without stressing it—canter the vertical two or three times.

Ride especially quietly to your first few canter jumps, so your horse stays relaxed. (If you run into problems at the jump, such as rushing or stopping,

see Lesson 15: Troubleshooting Tips, page 131.)

For the first two or three times, drop back to a trot before you turn to canter back over the fence, to reinforce the "quiet" message.

If your horse is heavy in your hands and hard to rebalance, circle until you've reestablished his rhythm and balance. When you can canter the vertical, circle, and canter back over it without losing balance for more than a stride or two, you're ready to progress.

Add a second fence four strides (60 feet) from the vertical; pace off the distance so it's normal for your horse. Now you have two opportunities to check your position and your horse's rhythm and balance.

If you don't feel confident enough to canter the line right away, trot the first fence and let your horse canter to the second. (Trotting into a line adds a stride to it, so the four will be a five.) After you've been through the line a few times, canter the first fence, too, then continue to the second fence in four strides.

When you're cantering both fences confidently, you'll have accomplished your aims: You'll have warmed up your horse without straining him, and you'll know all systems are working reliably.

If you're schooling at home, turn to "Lesson 14: Let's Jump A Course!" If you're at a show, take your preparation a step or two further by adding some components of the upcoming course.

For instance, if the course contains lines with long and short distances, close, then open up the distance in your practice line to check your horse's adjustability before you enter the ring.

This warm-up tests your own mental readiness for jumping. When your horse is limbered up and responsive, chances are you'll have the confidence to jump. And that's the point of all these lessons!

WARM-UP WISDOM

Some key points:

➤ **Let your horse be your guide.** For most horses, 15 minutes is enough to warm up muscles and ligaments, and get stiff joints moving. If your horse has a particular stiffness, or if he seems to respond better with more warm-up time, adjust your program accordingly.

➤ **Avoid a fight.** If you're working at home and he's very fresh, turn him out before you ride. (If you're at another barn or at a show, longe him.) He'll feel more relaxed, and you'll avoid a possible argument.

➤ **Check your horse's mood.** While you work, take note of your horse's mood. If he's resistant, spend plenty of time at the walk and trot to help him to a willing frame of mind; be sure he's comfortable before you advance to a canter.

➤ **Check *your* mood.** If you know you're out of sorts, recognize your poor humor and avoid blaming your horse for problems he didn't create. Tell yourself to relax, and work quietly through your warm-up until you feel more positive. (Simply riding will probably improve your mood!)

➤ **Check your position.** Every few minutes, run through your self-checklist, from your base of support to your eyes. If you're aware of a weak point—you stiffen through your shoulders or post with your hands, for example—check it even more frequently.

Let's Jump a Course!

IT'S TIME TO TAKE ALL THE CONFIDENCE YOU'VE
GAINED IN PREVIOUS LESSONS, AND PUT IT TOGETHER
ON A COURSE OF EIGHT FENCES.

You've been developing skills to ensure success both on the flat and over fences, by riding your horse in rhythm and in balance while following a very precise track.

In this lesson, you're going to draw on all these skills by jumping a course of six to eight fences. As always, we'll start slow, to ensure you build confidence, rather than erode it.

First, you'll properly warm up your horse, to ensure his responsiveness on a course. (Follow the warm-up outlined in Lesson 13, page 115.)

Next, you'll begin by setting your course as standards only. Later you'll add ground poles between the standards, and finally small jumps. Ready to begin? Then let's head off to the ring!

WHAT YOU'LL NEED:

➤ A level riding area with good footing, with enough space to set up a six-jump course.

➤ Enough standards and poles to set up a six-jump course, plus flower boxes if you have them. (If you don't have enough standards or poles, see Lesson 16: Get The Max From Minimum Jumps, page 141.)

Because your course's setup depends on the size of the workspace you have available, you'll have to be your own course designer. To help you, here are a few suggestions:

➤ Don't make your course too long, especially at first. Six jumps is plenty. (You can always repeat two jumps to make an eight-jump course.) A sample course is supplied in the diagram at right. Modify it as needed to fit your space. Include at least one wide turn and one sharper turn on your course.

➤ Leave just the standards on the course at first, so you can familiarize yourself with the track, without having to worry about the jumps. You can then add poles and/or flowerboxes, and finally, jumps.

➤ Try to make your course jumpable in both directions, so you get equal practice turning to the right and to the left. If that's

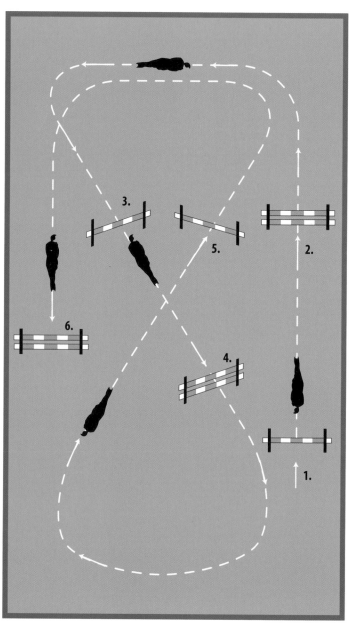

Sample Course

not possible, be certain to incorporate at least one right-hand and one left-hand turn.

➤ Set up unrelated distances, which will allow you to work off a rhythm rather than count strides. (Riding from rhythm will further develop your feel and your eye.) To do so, set single fences, or allow at least six strides—81 to 84 feet—between any two fences on a straight line.

1. To boost your confidence before you start jumping, trot through your "course" of standards first, to make sure you're really clear about your track. With an energetic working trot, guide your horse straight to the center of each pair of standards, using smooth, even turns, and riding through every corner—just as you'll do on a real course.

Maintain the same rhythm all the way through, counting one-two, one-two, if necessary, and adjusting the instant you feel your horse vary his cadence. Repeat from both directions, until you feel confident enough with your course to canter it.

2. When you feel ready, establish a rhythmic, balanced canter, maintaining light rein contact, and staying centered over your horse. Circle until you feel comfortable, then canter around your course track.

Keep your horse upright and balanced through the turns, looking ahead to your next set of standards, just as you did at the trot; ask for lead changes when necessary (see Lesson 6, page 61, if you encounter problems). Maintain your horse's rhythm over the entire track, adjusting instantly if he speeds up or slows down.

Repeat until you feel confident enough to canter a course over poles.

3. Now add your ground poles between the standards. Trot the pole-course first, just as you did without the poles. (Remember, this is just flatwork with poles in the way!) When you feel confident, negotiate it at the canter: Position your upper body slightly ahead of the vertical, and simply hold that same hip angle over each pole.

Ride your course of poles just as you've been riding over ground poles in all our work together. (See Lesson 5, page 55, if you need a refresher.) Nothing needs to change just because the poles are now set up in a course. Aim for a light contact all the time, with your horse stepping actively in front of your leg and soft in your hands—in other words, in *balance*.

4. If he leans on your hands and asks you to "carry" him to the poles…

5. …sit up and add leg while you squeeze, then release, with your fingers, to tell him in no uncertain terms that he's got to carry himself.

6. If your horse tries to speed up, bring your shoulders back and close your fingers until you re-establish the rhythm. Then immediately release your cues to reward him (otherwise, you'd "train" him to lean against your hands), and canter on.

WHEN YOU DON'T SEE A DISTANCE

You're cantering up to a jump on your course…and you see NOTHING! No distance. Zip. Zero. Nada! Now what? Relax—I have a plan for you.

Actually, I have two plans for you. I call them Plan A and Plan B. And they'll keep you clocking happily around a course if you just put them in action (or inaction, as the case may be). Here's how they work.

Plan A: This is the "everything's going right" plan. You see a distance. If it's a little long, you know from our previous lessons to lengthen. If it looks a little short, you know to shorten a little. If it looks ideal, you know to relax and enjoy it.

Plan B: Then there's the "I can't SEE it!" moment. Don't hit the panic button. If you can't see it, chances are there is no perfect distance. It happens. Avoid the temptation to hurl your body forward, grab your horse's mouth, or kick like a cowboy to find one. It won't work, and it *will* be ugly.

Instead, do nothing. That's right—it's the Zen approach to troubleshooting, and it works. Simply keep the balance. Keep the rhythm (counting one-two, one-two in your head if necessary to do so). And maintain your position in the tack by sitting absolutely still.

The worst thing that'll happen is your horse will pat the ground with his front feet and go over the jump from a tightish spot that'll look fine. No ugly running. No three-legged leaps. No gasps from the crowd. Nothing fear-inducing for you or your horse.

If you jump into a line like this, you may need to move up to make the distance, as you learned to do in Lesson 10, page 89. That's fine. Then you can settle in and enjoy the rest of the course!

7. If your horse slows down, immediately squeeze him (tapping him with the crop, if necessary) back into a lively canter. With time and practice, you'll develop a feel for these rhythm aberrations and correct them right away, to produce a balanced horse that canters in a tick-tock rhythm around an entire course. And, naturally, stays right on track!

Let's Jump It!

Next, replace the ground poles with very small jumps (tiny flower-boxes or a small stack of poles).

8. Ride these tiny jumps *exactly* as you rode the poles. Ride the rhythm (not the distance), and always keep your heels down to stay centered over your leg and prevent yourself from jumping ahead.

Of course, no matter how hard you try to ride the jumps as you rode the poles, your horse's attitude may change. If it does, you'll have to adapt:

9. If your horse sees a jump and begins to back off or slow down, avoid pumping your upper body to drive him toward the fence. Instead, keep your position quiet and centered, and make *him* keep his forward rhythm with a squeeze of your legs, as shown here, or a tap of your whip, or both. (For more information about problems on course, see Lesson 15: Troubleshooting Tips, page 131.) Troubleshooting Tips, page 131.)

10. Much more common is the horse that speeds up when he sees a jump, such as this horse is doing, regardless of how small the jump is. If yours does this, begin by asking yourself, "Why is he different over the jump from the way he was those 15 times over the pole?"

It may be that you've fallen into the trap of riding the jumps instead of the track; this makes you anxious, and your anxiety telegraphs right to your horse. What's more, pushing or pulling him (as you try to "find" a takeoff spot) will have him rushing to the jumps in self defense.

If your horse is taking over at the jumps, return to your simple poles and ride the exercise the right way—on soft contact, in a relaxed, steady rhythm—until you and your horse both settle down and forget any upsetting experiences.

This may take four times around the "pole course." It may take 40.

THE COMPETITIVE EDGE

You're at the in-gate at your next competition. Does anything change as you enter the ring to jump a course? Well, it shouldn't.

But if something in your head does, you have to clear your mind of any negative distractions or concerns. So, replace negative thoughts with positive, productive ones.

Easy for you to say, I'm sure you're thinking. But you really can retrain your brain to think positive, which will help you relax and ride with confidence at shows. You've learned all the tools in our lessons. Here's how to put them to use:

➤ **It's about the rhythm, stupid.** No, I'm not calling you stupid. But just like the economy effected a certain presidential election, you now know rhythm—or the lack of it—will make or break your course. Concentrate on establishing it on your opening canter circle, then remember to think: Rhythm first, distance second.

➤ **Ride what you've learned.** Keep your mind on the course, and remember where in the ring you'll have to make adjustments to your horse. (For instance, does he tend to slow in his corners? Be ready to make an adjustment *the instant* you feel him do so, just as you did at home.)

➤ **Ride with confidence.** As long as you've done your homework, by riding your horse in rhythm and in balance, accurately following preset tracks, and keeping your position as correct as possible, you can count on a lot of your riding responses to be automatic now. Have faith in yourself and your riding.

➤ **And, relax!** Before you enter the ring, take a couple of deep breaths. Tell yourself that you have all the time in the world. As you begin your course, open your mind to how everything should feel: you relaxed, calm, and balanced in the center of a horse that's also balanced and light in your hands; a dead-even canter that's neither lifeless nor hurried; no big moves at the jumps. Then, ride it that way!

➤ **Remember to breathe.** We're not pearl diving here. Breathing is not only recommended, it's encouraged. Keep breathing normally (you'd be amazed at how many riders hold their breath around an entire course) and you'll stay more relaxed. At home practice breathing when you land after each jump, and taking a deep breath in each corner.

You'll stay more relaxed, which will keep your horse more relaxed. Showing *is* supposed to be fun! And it will be, if you follow these tips.

11

fences, but the reward of a relaxed and easy performance will be well worth it.

11. Over the coming months, as your confidence builds, gradually raise the jumps until you're riding them at 2'6" to 3 feet. That'll be the only change to your course. You'll still sit quietly and ride him in metronome-like rhythm, up to…

12. …over, and away from each jump. That way, he—and you—will come to believe that jumping is no big deal. If you do run into any of the problems listed above (or any problems at all), drop back a level until you've worked through them, and only then start raising the height again, starting one jump at a time. (Also, see Lesson 15: Troubleshooting Tips, page 131.)

Above all, even as the jumps get higher, ride the rhythm and not the distance. And enjoy that ride, because you now have the confidence to do so.

Regardless, you've got to be sure that he's completely re-established his relaxed attitude over the poles before you try the jumps again. Then, when you do, add them one at a time, rather than going for all six or eight, to help keep him relaxed.

It may take weeks before you can finally ride a steady rhythm, on track, over all six or eight of your

12

Troubleshooting Tips

HERE ARE EIGHT COMMON PROBLEMS YOU MIGHT
FACE ON COURSE, AT HOME, OR IN THE SHOW RING
AND HOW TO DEAL WITH THEM.

When you visualize riding the perfect course, it's in a seamless canter in perfect rhythm from jump to jump. You're in total harmony with your horse as he flows from fence to fence.

But in reality, problems can—and do—occur. Everyone has them, even the pros. Your horse spooks or refuses. Loses rhythm on course. Or you lose security in the tack as the fences get bigger.

Stuff happens. In this lesson, I'm going to help you deal with it.

PROBLEM #1: **You lose your position over the fence.** You lose security in the tack when you jump. **Why it happens:** I can guarantee you're pinching your knee, pushing up off your toe, and losing depth in your heel. This position fault is also likely to make you jump ahead of your horse, so you disturb his balance on takeoff—a good way to make him worry and quicken to the jumps. **How to solve it:** Think about relaxing your entire leg and sinking your weight into your heels (as shown)—

THE PROBLEM

THE SOLUTION

before, over, and after each jump. (Avoid jamming your heel down, or you'll tense your leg). As long as your heel is below your toe, it will work. Then back up to cantering over a pole course, focusing on your position, before adding one fence at a time.

PROBLEM #2: You lose rhythm on course. Your horse speeds up, as this horse is doing, and/or slows down, rather than maintaining a metronome-like rhythm the whole way around.

Why it happens: It's likely pilot error. You may be chasing him (just as the rider, above right, is!), or taking back to try to "find" a distance. (For more information, see "When You Don't See A Distance," Lesson 14, page 127.) Here's what I mean:

If you're a "gunner"—that is, you finish your turn and immediately look for a distance that requires you to really step on the gas for a long spot—you're making the wrong decision by *overriding (increasing)* the rhythm.

On the other hand, if you're a "picker"—if you finish your turn and immediately start taking back to try to find a distance—you're making the wrong decision by *underriding (decreasing)* the rhythm. The distance you see will get shorter and shorter until you've run your horse up underneath the fence.

How to solve it: If you're a "gunner," just sit quietly (as shown above), keep the rhythm steady, and pass that "yahoo" option by. You'll eventually see a better option as your horse meets the fence perfectly by adding one more quiet stride.

THE PROBLEM

THE SOLUTION

If you're a picker, create a better distance by loosening up and letting his canter continue forward, in the same rhythm, out of the turn. Concentrate on the rhythm, and *ride your horse every step of the way* to maintain it. Be prepared to change your tactics as needed.

PROBLEM #3: Your horse stops at a fence. You're cantering along thinking everything's fine, and suddenly your horse slams on the brakes!

Why it happens: Usually it's one of three reasons—your horse is uncomfortable with the distance; he had to make a big effort over the previous fence, perhaps due to a bad distance, which has eroded his confidence; or he's spooked by the jump itself.

How to solve it: If you think he stopped because of a lack of distance, or a lack of confidence, avoid getting faster and more aggressive—it's counter-

THE PROBLEM

productive. You need to build his confidence, not shatter it. Instead, get reorganized. Re-establish a rhythmic, balanced, energetic canter, in which your horse is carrying himself, neither pulling nor sucking back against your aids. (This may take one circle, or 10.)

Take a deep breath, stay relaxed, and ride him confidently back to the fence, waiting for a good, comfortable distance to come up (as shown at right). When he's able to jump from a comfortable distance, chances are he will.

If, however, you rode him to a good distance and he still stopped, chances are he's seeing horse-eating monsters in that particular fence. You need to ride a bit more aggressively, to convince him he *can* jump it. By that, I don't mean faster or harder, which would get him strung out, worried, and wreck your chances of finding a comfortable distance to make it easy for him.

THE SOLUTION

THE PROBLEM

I *do* mean taking a greater feel of his mouth, and using more leg than you did the first time, to package him between your aids, so you create a "chute" through which to drive him straight to the jump—and block off any escape routes. (You taking more control will also fuel his confidence.)

Subtly shift your shoulders *slightly* back—but keep them ahead of your hips so your body angle remains forward—and drop your weight lightly into your seat and legs to drive him forward smoothly. He'll have only one option: to maintain a forward stride straight to the base of the jump.

If he hesitates when he gets there, cluck. If he needs additional encouragement, touch him with your spurs. If he needs still more, tap him with the stick behind your leg (inset), to reinforce your "go!" message. Give him a big pat after he jumps the scary fence, to reward his bravery.

If your horse's lack of confidence has inflamed your own, ask a stronger, more confident rider (such as a trainer) to school your horse over the jump. If that's not possible, lower the fence. Walk your horse up to it, and let him stand there until he lowers his head and sniffs it. Then pick up an energetic working trot, and trot over it.

If your problem has occurred in a line, try trotting in and cantering out, or jumping each fence separately, before stringing them together in a canter line. Add a stride, if needed, the first time you canter the line. You can open up your horse's step when you both feel more confident.

PROBLEM #4: Your horse sucks back at new fences. Your horse gives new or unusual jumps a hard look as he approaches them, slowing his step and literally sucking back with his body as he looks—and ruining your course flow!

Why it happens: Some horses naturally have a lot of "look." It can make them careful jumpers, but it means when you approach a new fence (or one with,

THE PROBLEM

THE SOLUTION

say, flower boxes, if your horse hates flower boxes), you need to be thinking proactively, rather than reactively.

How to solve it: Repetition usually solves this "lookiness." The more your horse sees each jump, the less he'll worry about it. If you show and your horse is a looker when he first sees the jumps, recruit a good pro to pilot him around the course in a schooling round. If that's not possible, see "How to solve it," under "Problem #3: Your horse stops at a fence," page 134.

PROBLEM #5:

Your horse is spooky. Your horse seems to see lions and tigers and bears behind every show-ring banner,

standard, water cooler, or judge's stand at shows, or behind trashcans and other everyday objects at home. You can't maintain a seamless rhythm on course when he occasionally—and unexpectedly—levitates to one side or the other!

Why it happens: He may be green, and will improve with mileage. Or he may naturally be spooky. Either way, you need to learn to deal with it.

How to solve it: A horse that's allowed to focus fully on something that scares him is likely to implode as he passes it. So the instant you see a spooky object, and/or feel an impending spook, subtly redirect your horse's attention away from the "monster," as our rider is doing in the "solution" photo.

Say the object of his fear is on your left. Apply slight right-rein pressure, to tip his head away, and to send a "listen to me!" message. At the same time, close your right leg at the girth to keep him moving on a straight track. You'll minimize the risk of an outburst. And, if you're showing, your subtle aids won't call attention to the problem. (Note: If your horse is typically spooky when he's fresh—and many are—longe him or turn him out to settle him, before you ride or show.)

PROBLEM #6: Too strong on course. Your horse gets stronger and stronger as you navigate a course.

Why it happens: You may have revved him up over fences by kicking hard to long distances, riding tense and nervous (a problem we should've solved with the lessons in this book), or allowing him to build, by not maintaining your rhythm. Or, he may be one of those horses that simply gets "game" when he sees an arena full of jumps (especially at a show).

How to solve it: Use these guidelines.

➤ Keep your head and eyes up, sitting slightly more upright than your normal two-point, as our rider is demonstrating in the "solution" photo on this page. If you were to look down and tip your shoulders forward, you'd be fueling his speed like a jockey on a racehorse.

➤ Use your corners after diagonal lines, and the ends of the ring after outside lines, to sit up, rebal-

THE PROBLEM

THE SOLUTION

ance, and regain your rhythm. Ride deep into the corners; the arena railing will naturally cause your horse to tap his brakes. (Always make this correction in the five or six strides *after* a fence, not the five or six strides *before* the next one.)

➤ Do your homework. The more broke your horse is

THE PROBLEM

THE SOLUTION

at home, the more control you'll have on course at a show. That, my friends, builds confidence!

➤ If your horse only wakes up when you show, bring him down to a walk, on loose contact, for a few steps after trotting into the ring, before asking him to canter. This is acceptable in either the hunter or jumper ring, and allows him (and you) to relax a few moments before you begin your course.

➤ At shows (and at home), resist the temptation to start out extra slow (a *common* mistake) at the canter. You'd only force him to speed up as he tries to compensate for a lack of power and energy to the fences. Instead, use your opening circle to establish the exact pace and rhythm you want on course—just like you've learned to do at home.

PROBLEM #7:

Losing balance in the turn. Rather than your horse staying upright between your reins and legs, he (or you) leans inward (see the rider in the photo) or bows outward (see the horse in the photo!).

Why it happens: A lot of riders slide slightly to the outside or inside of the saddle around turns, shifting more and more as the turn gets sharper. Unless your position is completely secure, with your balance centered over your legs and your heels down, this is likely to happen to you, too. The result? You wreck your horse's balance, and his rhythm, and your track, making it difficult to find a good distance.

How to solve it: Keep your weight evenly distributed over both stirrups to stay centered above your horse, which will encourage him to stay centered and balanced beneath you. Think of the way a centerboard in a sailboat works to prevent the boat from tipping over. Imagine your horse's legs are an extension of your legs, and together they form the centerboard; your upper body is the sail. If they all line up, you'll stay balanced, just as a sailboat stays afloat.

Practice at home, by making a "harder" turn—one that comes up sooner—between two jumps. Using cones or standards as markers, try turning 50 feet from the jumps; then gradually move your markers closer to the jumps until you are able to jump, balance yourself and your horse, then look for and follow your track around a turn that's only 35 or 40 feet away. Keep your hip angle slightly closed throughout, letting your horse close it further over the jumps.

Once your position is secure and balanced enough that you can stay "in touch" with your horse as you guide him on a hard-turning track, you can be confident about almost any turning question that will come up on course.

PROBLEM #8:

The drifter. Your horse has a tendency to drift off your track as he approaches his fences, veering leftward or rightward.

8

THE PROBLEM

THE SOLUTION

Why it happens: You're not keeping your horse centered between your rein-and-leg "chute"—and on your track. And/or, he may be green and a bit wiggly, and your reaction times aren't fast enough to repackage him to *keep* him on track. This is key: Not only is drifting unsightly and a quick way to erode a good distance, but it also can cause problems in a line. It'll make the line ride longer by increasing the distance between one jump and the next. That can hurt if your horse is short-strided.

How to solve it: Drifters typically are consistent about direction. Let's say your horse tends to veer to the right, especially in lines, as the horse is doing on page 139. As you canter to the first jump, use your leg and rein aids as necessary, to guide him to its center. A horse that jumps into a line centered has less room to drift.

The instant his front feet touch the ground, close your right leg on the "drift" side and apply a *slight* opening left rein (no more than an inch or two), to redirect his front end opposite the drift. Your closed leg blocks movement in that direction; the opening rein sends a subtle "stay-straight" message.

You'll then reach the second fence centered; the line will have ridden more easily because your horse was straight. At home and in show warm-ups, physically and mentally block your horse's drift, using ground-pole barriers. Horses naturally tend to avoid contact with any perceived barriers. Warming up with them will keep your horse thinking "straight" when you jump a course.

Set up a pole before and after a warm-up fence, perpendicular to and just inside the standards, on the side to which he drifts. (You may need several poles for inside a line.) Start with them just inside the standard until he gets used to seeing them. Then roll them to just outside the jumps' and line's center, to mentally "squeeze" him to the center.

Your horse will soon "get it," staying centered between your reins and legs with no corrective aids from you. That's the mindset you want him to carry on course, be it at home or in the show ring.

BONUS CHAPTER!

Get the Max from Minimum Jumps

ARRANGE TWO TO FOUR JUMPS IN A FEW DIFFERENT WAYS, AND YOU CAN
MASTER NEARLY ALL THE SKILLS YOU AND YOUR HUNTER, JUMPER, EVENTER, OR
"EQ" HORSE NEED ON COURSE—AND RATCHET UP YOUR CONFIDENCE EVEN MORE.

You want on-course experience but can't afford the expense of a full course of jumps—and don't have the arena to hold them anyway. I'll show you how you can use just two to four jumps to build strong basics and polish such skills as:

- ➤ Rhythm
- ➤ Distances
- ➤ Diagonal and bending lines
- ➤ Straight approaches
- ➤ Pace

- ➤ Adjustability
- ➤ Turns
- ➤ "Skinny" jumps
- ➤ And even flying changes

Along the way, you'll correct one-sidedness, learn how to influence the lead your horse lands on.... The benefits just keep coming.

You can set up the exercises I'll be showing you in almost any work area, big or small—100 feet by 125 feet would be ideal, but less will do. In fact, though I don't encourage you to go much narrower, you can definitely shorten things up to fit in a small dressage arena.

I've arranged the exercises from easiest to most challenging. Be sure you're completely confident riding the easier ones before you step up the challenge. Before you start, be sure to check my general guidelines in the "Details, Details" box at right. See also the "Why It Works" box, below. And, warm up your horse as you learned in Lesson 13, page 115.

WHY IT WORKS

How come less can be best when it comes to fences? It's because jumping a reduced number on a miniature course enables you to:

➤ **Focus.** They let you focus on one specific skill at a time, without the pressure of riding a full course.

➤ **Relax.** The simplicity, rhythm, and repetition can get so mesmerizing that you and your horse go "phewwwww," take the big, deep breath that's so essential to thinking while riding, and relax.

➤ **Dig in.** Simplicity encourages you to dig into the details of what you do right, what you tend to let slide and need to work on, and what so easily gets lost or falls apart on course, like position or pace.

➤ **Play the options.** You have tons of options. Do an exercise once so you zero in on a specific element; let it flow a couple of times to get the feel of eight consecutive fences; experiment by reversing a pattern or juggling the order of fences, focus one time on keeping your elbows in and another time on your horse's bend....

➤ **And build...confidence!** When the time does come to ride a course, you'll have worked through all its individual elements at home. You'll be able to confidently dissect the course in front of you as a doable sequence of related "been there, done that" moments.

EXERCISE 1: THE FOUR-FENCE COURSE

What you'll learn: Rhythm; breathing (and thinking clearly) on course; how to find distances that work; looking in and holding out on a turn ("inside leg to outside rein"); staying straight on the track; and how to regroup when things fall apart!

Setup: Arrange four jumps in the middle of your work space, as shown in the diagram below, with standards close or touching, fences 2 and 3 at right angles, and enough room top and bottom for comfortable turns.

Set fences 1 and 4 inside the track so you can canter

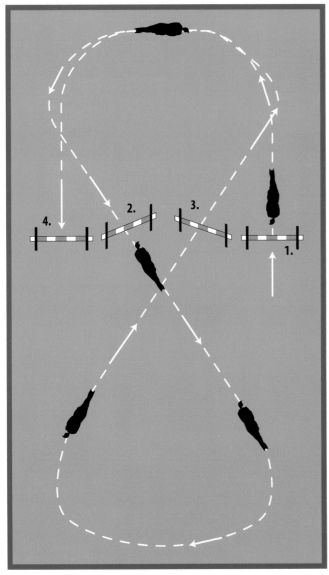

Exercise 1: The Four-Fence Course

DETAILS, DETAILS

➤ Recruit a knowledgeable helper to adjust your jumps and keep an eye on your position.

➤ Set fences so you can jump in either direction.

➤ Practice first with empty standards (jump cups removed for safety), to get a feel for the pattern, the jumping efforts required, and what maintaining a flowing, even pace requires. Then add poles on the ground, crossrails, and so on. Gradually—always within your comfort level—work up to the height you expect to jump at a show.

➤ At each new level, trot or canter one jump at a time, walk the turn, and then trot or canter the next jump until you and your horse are relaxed and confident enough to trot or canter the entire pattern.

➤ As always, keep things rhythmic—that's what creates the consistent stride that allows you to see a distance. And if you have a choice, take a quieter distance (longer encourages your horse to speed up). Take a deep breath after every jump, and use the ends of the ring to check: "Do I still have pace and rhythm? Do I need to rebalance? Do I need to stop?"

➤ If you lose position or focus, walk and regroup. If your horse takes over on the approach, or gets quick off the ground or strong on landing, walk or halt; if he really takes over, halt and back up. (And turn to Lesson 15: "Troubleshooting Tips," Problem #6, page 137.) Only push yourself to keep going and make the fix "in motion" when you're comfortable doing so.

➤ Jump for no more than 20 or 30 minutes, with frequent breaks. Do one exercise per session, even if it's a piece of cake. If you have to challenge yourself, do it by experimenting: Reverse the pattern. Make earlier turns and shorter approaches. Raise the jumps. Do spreads or triple bars. Come on! Try something new! That's half the fun!

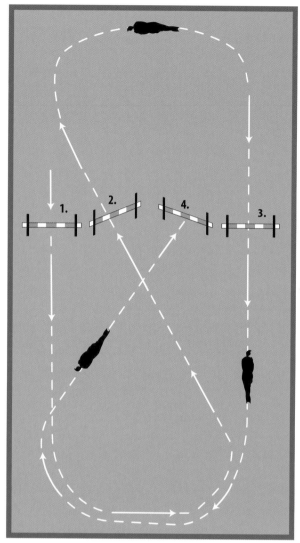

Bonus: Optional Route

to where you're going. As you approach the midpoint of the short side at the base of the diagram, look at the center of fence 1 so you make a flowing corner and get your horse straight to the fence.

If, like some of my students, you tend to fiddle with your horse's stride when you look at the fence, lift your eye and focus on a point at the end of the ring directly in line with the center of the fence.

1A. Jump the center, land straight, and immediately use the fairly roomy space ahead to take a deep breath and ask, "Is my horse a little heavy? Has our pace increased because of the jump?"

If so, ask him to come back by getting deeper in your tack: Sink your seat bones so that they just touch the saddle, drop more weight into your heels, and bring your shoulders back an inch or so.

If he ignores your aids, regroup on a circle, or by walking, halting (correcting any lack of straightness as you close your hand), and, if necessary, adding a reinback (and make a mental note to do more flat-work to teach him to be adjustable to your aids).

1B. Ride straight to the end—if you let your horse cut in here, he'll bulge out on the next turn—and do a

down the long sides without jumping. (Fence 4 is an optional extra; leave it out if you don't have enough material or space.)

The pattern (see page 143)**_:_**
a. Canter up to fence 1 on the left lead.
b. Turn down to 2 on a diagonal line.
c. Turn back around to the right to 3.
d. And turn left and come down to 4.

How to ride it:

In two-point position—seat just out of the saddle, as in the "up" phase of posting trot—establish a medium canter pace on a left-lead circle. Look up and ahead

1B

1C

➤ If your horse cuts in or bulges out on the turns, circle or walk to fix the problem.

➤ If he builds pace and his temperament changes from relaxed to strong, ask yourself, "Am I doing something to disrupt the rhythm, upset him, and make him speed up?" Check (and remind your helper to watch for you) that you're not riding off your hands, catching him in the mouth, inadvertently driving him forward with your seat or clamped legs, going for long distances, or making big moves with your upper body.

➤ If you do get a bad distance, ask yourself what changed. Did you lean forward up his neck? Grab or totally let go with your leg? Take away his stride with nervous hands? Or did your track change? Did you look late and turn late, a stride after you saw the center of the fence? Or early, anticipating the turn? Try drawing a line on the ground, from the center of the jump back to the corner, to help you identify the track—but don't start looking down.

➤ If he tends to land to the right or left of the track, guide him back with both reins and a little leg on the drift side—without increasing the canter.

simple or flying change if necessary. Look and turn left, as shown, and stay out on the rail until you see the center of fence 2's top rail.

You want to be able to see that point and still fit in as many *straight* strides as possible between your turn and the jump. (Ride it a few times and you'll know exactly where to turn to arrive in four, five, or however many straight strides your workspace allows.)

If you need to make a correction—because your horse accelerates or slows down through the turn—do it smoothly, closing your hand or leg exactly as you would on the flat to maintain pace and rhythm.

1C. What about a distance? Do not try to create one. If you just maintain your balanced position and your horse's rhythm (so every stride is the same), and ride a straight approach, a distance will be there.

Just relax and believe in your skills—rhythm, pace, and straightness—and in your horse's ability to jump the jump without your legging him off the ground or making any sort of move at him with your body.

1D. Wait until you're confident he's going to jump; about three or four strides away, raise your eyes from the top of the jump to a focal point at the end of your work area (you'll still see the jump in your peripheral vision), and let the distance happen. By sitting quietly and looking up, you'll help him jump more easily and be more rideable on the other side.

Land, *breathe*, then collect and balance your horse so he can maintain pace and flow…

1E. …on the circle-back turn to the right: Sink into your tack, bring your shoulders back, close your hand if necessary (but remember, the tighter the turn, the more he'll come back, even if you do nothing), and look around the turn toward fence 3 so you can plan a smooth approach with as many straight strides as possible.

And remind yourself: "For this—for every—turn, I use both reins and both legs, but my *stronger* aids are my pushing-out inside leg and my receiving outside rein." Of course, depending on your horse, you may need a strong outside leg and rein to bring him around the turn, or barely any.

1F. Jump 3, land, breathe, and run a quick mental check: "Is my horse on his front end? Am I losing position or

focus? Should I walk, regroup, and begin again? Or can I continue on?" If you can, flow on around the turn to 4…

1G. …and finish your "mini" course. If things are going well after fence 4, ride through the end of the ring, and repeat the entire pattern to get a good feel of a flowing eight jumps. Or develop your turning skills by reversing the pattern, riding down fence 1, up fence 3, down fence 4, and up fence 2. Get a bit more "equitation-y" by cutting off the ends of the ring for even tighter turns from 1 to 3 and 4 to 2.

As you work through each of these options, monitor the quality of your ride. After two or three jumps, ask yourself: Does my horse have the same pace he had coming to 1? Is he rushing toward the barn (or creeping away from it)? Do I need to circle before continuing? Do I need to walk (or halt on a straight line)? Do I need to do *anything*? Or can I just relax and enjoy the ride?"

EXERCISE 2: LINES AND SINGLES

What you'll learn: Riding a line; regrouping afterward; going from a diagonal line to a diagonal single; consistency.

Setup: Arrange three jumps in the middle of your work area as shown in the diagram on page 148, with fences 1 and 2 forming one diagonal line (set them four or six strides apart, depending on the space you have—see page 103 for measurements). Set fence 3 as a single jump on the other diagonal. Have the standards for fences 1 and 3 close or touching, if needed for space.

The pattern:

a. You'll canter a right-lead turn, then down to and through the diagonal line.

b. You'll land and turn left.

c. Then you'll come up the second diagonal to the single fence 3.

How to ride it: I've already given you most of the pattern-riding routine in Exercise 1, so I'll just emphasize that here, in addition to all the landing and regrouping skills we've talked about, the big deal is to make sure everything stays *consistent*.

You don't want to be slow around the end, flying down the line, and accelerating even more to the single (especially if you have a hope of repeating the pattern). And even though you do have some room after the line, it's a fairly small space in which to land, breathe, make sure your horse hasn't picked up speed, do something about it if he has, and prepare for the change and the left turn to fence 3—all the while maintaining that nice solid rhythm.

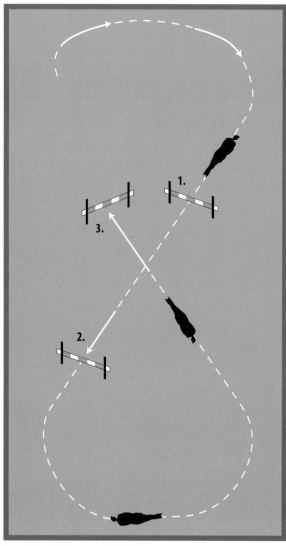

Exercise 2: Lines and Singles

On-course alert: If your horse picks up speed in the line, smoothly sink deeper into your tack and take his mouth more firmly for a couple of strides. On landing, check what you have and use whichever regrouping exercise—circle, halt on a straight line—seems appropriate. Then enjoy!

EXERCISE 3: ANGLING FOR A DISTANCE

What you'll learn: Jumping at an angle; eye control; keeping your horse straight; riding forward out of the turn when you don't have a specific number of strides; and along the way, great troubleshooting skills and how to control a horse that "takes over" in the approach.

Setup: Arrange two jumps as shown in the diagram at right, placing them to one side of the middle of your work area and far from the ends to leave room for turns and approaches. You can use a four- (60 feet), five- (72 feet), or six-stride (84 feet) line, depending on space. The longer the line, the gentler the angle of approach to each fence.

I like to leave room for at least four strides between each fence and the ends of the ring. If your space is too tight for that, set just one jump halfway down your work area, and jump it using the same figure-eight pattern.

The pattern:
a. Ride a left-lead canter down the long side of your work area, to the outside of the two jumps.
b. Turn left to come snugly past fence 2.
c. Ride an angled track to the center of fence 1.
d. Jump on an angle.
e. Turn to the right, ride an angled track to fence 2, and jump it on an angle.

How to ride it:
These jumps come up pretty quickly, so start your horse off a little slowly with quiet schooling distances and a fairly short release. (As a general rule the hotter he is, the quieter your ride should be.)

As he relaxes into the rhythm and flow, reward him by gradually getting a little looser in your arm, softening to allow him to be more forward until he's traveling around the pattern with a very light contact—the way every horse should.

If your horse is of the quick variety and/or has very little mouth, use the exercise right away to develop a mouth and reliable control by trotting to each fence and stopping (and backing if you need to) on a straight line after each landing.

3A. If control is not a big issue, start at the canter. Pick up the left lead on the long side. Ride a balanced, rhythmic left turn. As you begin your turn,

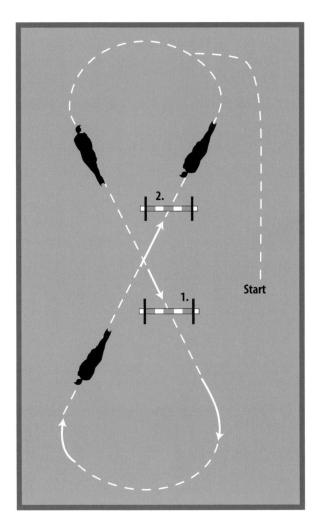

Exercise 3: Angling for a Distance

look at the center of fence 1 (or, if you fidget when you dial in on fences, beyond it). Come out of the turn on a straight line, shaving your track close to fence 2's standard so your jumping angle at fence 1 is as shallow and inviting as possible.

Ride to a quiet distance. If your horse tends to be hot, soften for the airborne moment of each stride, then close your fingers more firmly again until you can softly follow his mouth.

As you near fence 1, raise your focus to a point at the end of your ring and use it to keep your horse dead straight on the angled track…

3B. … as you jump the fence. On landing, regroup as necessary, rebalancing the canter, coming back to the walk, even stopping and backing. Then quietly ride the turn through the end of the ring. As you approach the corner, continue to use inside leg and outside rein to ensure straightness. Through the corner, close your outside rein and leg, and keep just enough inside leg to give him something to turn around. Then, as you come out of the corner, slightly open your inside rein to influence the turn.

3C. Approach fence 2 on an angled track, maintaining your rhythm and balance, and waiting…

3D. …for the fence to come to you. Then enjoy the benefit—a lovely jump, taken by a confident horse and rider. And there will be many more to come, thanks to the lessons you learned in this book. Good luck!